MY CRAZY LOVE

FOR

Alcoholics

HOW I STOPPED BLAMING THEM AND BEGAN
MY OWN JOURNEY OF SERENITY

BY
BELINDA SLONE ELLIOTT

Λ⊢
Avonlea House

Avonlea House Publishing
333 East Center St
Marion, OH 43302
www.avonleahousepublishing.com

Publisher's Note: Each story is a product of the author's interpretation. Locales and public names are sometimes used for atmospheric purposes. Any resemblance to actual people, living or dead, or to businesses, companies, events, institutions, or locales is completely coincidental.

Cover Art by Mason McCall

My Crazy Love for Alcoholics/Belinda Slone Elliott – 2nd ed.
ISBN 978-0-6928-54969

THIS BOOK IS DEDICATED TO

The memory of my student and friend from
Plano, TX

BENJAMIN JACKSON

Who left this world for the next too soon!

ABOUT THE AUTHOR

Belinda Slone Elliott has been a teacher in public school, Christian school, driving school, preschool, Sunday school, women's Bible studies and has tutored over fifty students.

She currently lives in Elyria, Ohio. She was born in Raven, Kentucky, but her family moved to Ohio for better employment when she was three. Belinda was educated at Keystone High School in LaGrange, Ohio, and Baldwin-Wallace College in Berea, Ohio, with a BS in ED degree emphasizing language arts. She did Master's level studies as well. Her greatest professional accomplishment was founding a dream-come-true school with a business partner.

Belinda's single greatest accomplishment in life is raising one incredible son who gave her an amazing daughter-in-law and two adorable grandchildren. She was married once for five years and again for thirty years. Thanks to both marriages, she enjoyed two great blessings: her family and her teaching career.

Belinda is available to speak to your group of any size.

CONTACT: elliottbelinda73@gmail.com

Foreword

PLEASE READ THIS!!

Most people don't read these parts of books. Thanks for being different.

This book is not intended to be a condemnation of alcoholics and the people who love them. Quite the opposite! It is intended to be only my story, my experience of loving alcoholics and becoming sick – emotionally and spiritually – and how I finally found sanity out of all the chaos in a simple way of life. The biblical principles and twelve-step principles which I believe have helped me may also help someone else.

I want to share the message, share my experience, and how I found strength and hope. If you can relate to my story and feel encouraged, great. If not, perhaps you can pass this book on to someone else? You don't need to agree with everything I say. It's MY experience, perhaps not yours. Take what you like and leave the rest.

The Bible and the Twelve Steps are genius principles for living life to the fullest. They are parallel – one simply showed me how to apply the principles of the other. I owe a debt of gratitude to both. I have never been happier in my life! John 10:10 says, "I [Jesus] have come that you may have LIFE, and that more abundantly." LIFE! Full life as God intended – with sanity, serenity, simplicity, and service to others – these make life overflowing with abundant happiness.

I am just an ordinary person who loves alcoholics, attracted to them like a moth to a flame. I am not an expert on anything. I am just striving to be the person God created me to be, the sum total of my experiences, choices, and decisions, good and bad.

If I sound "preachy" or lecturing, forgive me; it's just my style. <u>Nothing I have said in this book should be taken authoritatively for your life's journey.</u> The principles of AA and Al-Anon have been effective in my life. They may help you, too. This book was begun as a journal - a therapeutic tool for my own recovery from distorted thinking. I do NOT have all the answers.

I am on a journey of serenity, genuine daily peace. The journey will not end until I die. The serenity I seek is found along the way like beautiful flowers I am free to pick. But like flowers which may only stay fresh for a day, I need to keep picking more and more of them every day as I keep moving along my journey.

Serenity is not a destination; serenity IS the journey. Join me on this journey, if you dare!

How It All Began

It was just a joke.

My brother has always enjoyed teasing me; "yanking my chain" he calls it.

I fell asleep watching a movie. He was annoyed. My friend and I were visiting him in Florida for ten days and he was trying to be a good host, but I was tired. There I was, asleep sitting up, head back on the couch, mouth open, left arm extended, a chain which begged to be yanked.

He couldn't resist. Shave cream in my palm and a tickling feather under my nose – what a perfect set-up! A few seconds later I jumped up, still half asleep, smearing shave cream all over my head, while he laughed hysterically, trying to explain to me what was going on.

Seconds later, as I began to wake up, I suddenly got it! "I - did - it - to - myself?" I whined slowly and sleepily in disbelief.

And so I learned the greatest lesson of my life.

I DID IT ALL TO MYSELF!

ALL THE MISERY, SUFFERING, UNHAPPINESS, DISCOMFORT, IRRITATION – YOU NAME IT – I DID IT ALL TO MYSELF.

I just didn't know it for a long time . . . until a recovered alcoholic friend suggested kindly that perhaps I was "sicker than that crazy husband" of mine. I had been complaining about for months – and he WAS sick!

It hurt my feelings to hear such an idea, but I was already on a journey of self-discovery, and I really respected my friend, so I gave it some thought. Something WAS wrong with me. Two failed marriages to men I thought were very different.

I had begun my journey, if only with the baby step of recognizing and admitting I had a problem. But I had been stuck for years playing the "Blame Game" – my parents, my brother, my uncles, my cousins, my church's legalistic rules, my first husband's addictions, my southern heritage, my second husband and his verbal abuse, PMS, stress, my business partner, a chemical imbalance, clinical depression – my knowing whom or what to BLAME NEVER CURED THE PROBLEM. I was still sick – only at least now I knew it.

God bless my family doctor who wisely suggested that I should read a book his great uncle had written entitled, appropriately, *You Can't Make Me Angry*. I was stunned! Why did he think I needed a book with such a title? He explained that his uncle's and aunt's story was featured in the AA Big Book, and perhaps it would help me deal with my husband. Huh? Problem! Neither my husband nor I was a drinker. My doctor knew us both well, however, and because I trusted my doctor so much, I decided to buy the book and read it.

He also suggested that I had a decision to make with four options: either stay with the man and continue to be unhappy, leave him and continue to be unhappy, stay with him and be happy, or leave him and be happy. I easily chose the last option after my husband screamed at me in a rage that he wanted to kill me.

And that's basically how this journey of serenity began – with the awareness of a problem that only I could change, the humility to admit my life was a mess and I could not fix it, and the need for help from a Power greater than any human power.

Warning: I am still on this journey. There is no end. The journey itself IS my destiny; the journey IS the source of my serenity. Serenity is not a far-off goal I must work hard to reach some day. Serenity is mine for the taking TODAY.

This is just a collection of essays. Some of the essays may seem to repeat the same ideas. That's on purpose for two reasons: repetition is a good way to learn, and the principles of this book are just that – principles, not rules – and these principles are like the petals of flowers – "similarly different" – and all connected, overlapping.

What I love about the slogans and principles of AA and Al-Anon is that they are applicable to so many situations. I also include many Bible references. I love the Bible, and I believe its principles are parallel to the twelve steps of AA and Al-Anon. I pray God will encourage you through these writings.

Part Two of How it All Began

"Twelve steps. Wow!" I thought to myself, "I can do that. Twelve months in a year, one step per month. Cool. I can lick this problem in about a year, and maybe I can double time it and do it in six months. I'm a smart person, a quick learner, a good student in school . . ." with a lifetime of distorted thinking just like that!

I live in a world of fast food and instant answers, three reasons, five causes, thirty days, quick fixes for everything imaginable. "Lose that ugly belly in 10 days without dieting, without exercise! Send us $19.95 plus handling today and we will double the offer . . ."

"Just put your hand on the TV screen, send us $20.00, and all your prayers will be answered." Not to question the man's motives, but the implication, sometimes actually stated, was that you would also have the ability . . . no, not just the ability, the mandate . . . to change the world! *Powerful stuff, huh?* And I only wanted to change one man!

Much of my distorted thinking, my "IC" as I like to call it (from the word alcohol-ic), began in my childhood. It never occurred to me to blame my parents until a counselor asked me how my childhood was. I answered, "It was great." I later asked my brother his opinion of our childhood, and he said just the opposite.

My counselor asked me, "How could two wonderful parents raise two such dysfunctional children?" I eagerly began blaming my parents for much of what was wrong in my life. I had already been married and divorced and married again. I was miserable; my second marriage was a disaster, and I was afraid to tell anyone.

My difficulties DID begin in my family of origin as all our defects of character do. It IS a fact of life and of our culture. We ARE raised by flawed, imperfect parents because they were raised by flawed, imperfect parents. It is a generational problem – a family disease, and if that word "disease" is bothersome, just think of it as an unpleasant situation. "Dis" means "lacking" and "ease" means "comfort" – disease simply "lacking comfort."

The problem for me, and perhaps for many others, was that I got stuck on BLAME. Blaming only reveals our arrogance, our lack of humility, our childish ingratitude, our utter immaturity; and, when it takes root, it grows into resentment, bitterness, anger, and unholy martyrdom.

Some of my distorted thinking developed as a result of expecting God to reward me for "being a good girl" with all the good things in life I had always wanted. As a teenager, believe me, I wanted rewards! For my good behavior and good grades, I wanted a handsome, sexy, loving husband who would make a good living, give me four beautiful and smart children [2 boys, 2 girls, perfect], build our dream house on a sloping country acre with a little creek running alongside it, a stand of feathery honey locust trees in the front yard, a woodsy split-rail fence, a lush vegetable garden, a pristine pond, a walk-out basement family room with a fieldstone fireplace, stacks of firewood beside the door . . . and we would indeed have had all that and lived there happily to this very day but for one problem. Alcohol. Simple. If only he would have stopped drinking that stuff. It was all his fault . . . and God was not being fair. What kind of a reward was THIS?

More distorted thinking – all my unhappiness, all the problems in my life were his fault. Blame Game continues, Level Two. It gets complicated now, but husband #1 made it easy to blame him, after all. Everyone could see he was a problem drinker, and I was "a good girl who deserved only the best." Everyone said so! I was an enthusiastic college student preparing for a teaching career, a faithful church member, and I had never been in serious trouble in school or at home.

The good girl attracted to the rebel, literally to the tune of *"He's a rebel and he'll never be any good, he's a rebel cause he doesn't do what he should, but just because he doesn't do what everyone else does, that's no reason why we can't share love."* [written by Gene Pitney and sung by the Crystals]

No girl could have been more devoted to a guy who deserved it less. As a Marine, he spent 13 months in Vietnam where I wrote to him every single day, turning down dates at college because I was being "faithful." But life was not turning out the way I had dreamed it would, the way I had expected, the way GOD was supposed to make it work out for me – "the good girl rewarded."

What to do? maybe I could love him more unconditionally, assure him that I would never leave him, never stop loving him no matter what? And I did that. I told him, "There is nothing you can ever do or say that can make me stop loving you." WOW! Who can resist a love and devotion like that? An alcoholic can, that's who. An AA friend of mine says often, "Threaten to leave an alcoholic if he doesn't stop drinking, leave him, and he will keep drinking. Tell him he will die if he doesn't stop, and he will die. Drinking is what an alcoholic is driven to do." He drank daily, came home very late most nights, and in sober morning moments, begged me to forgive him, promising me he would never do "that" again. At the time I didn't really believe him, but I loved him and I wanted so badly to believe him.

I used to look back and assert that I would have married him again . . . if I knew that I would have a terrific son, a beautiful daughter-in-law, and two fantastic grandchildren because of that marriage. The scariest thing is, not knowing that, I would still have married him again as long as I WAS THE SAME PERSON. The determining factor in my unhappiness was ME, not him or his drinking or an unfair God or anything else I blamed. (By the way, he is sober now, a good Christian man, and I am proud of him.)

I believe in Romans 8:28-29 which says that, for believers, everything works together for good, ultimately to accomplish God's perfect plan – to conform us to His image, to grow us up. God is less concerned about solving my problems, having me make the right decisions, being "perfect" . . . than He is concerned about achieving His purpose in my life.

Realizing that fact hurt my feelings at first! God did not want to solve all my problems? God wasn't going to grant all my prayer-wishes – my laundry list of expected rewards for my good behavior? Then how could I ever get through this life? Someone had to help me . . . and Someone did! My Higher Power whom I call God, Jesus Christ, and wonderful friends in AA and Al-Anon groups.

A Note About the God of My Understanding

In the beginning, I had a real problem with the AA third step: *"Made a decision to turn my will and my life over to the care of God as I understood Him."* I have always been a spiritual person and a believer in Jesus Christ since I was a teenager, but the idea of calling him my 'higher power" seemed disrespectful, and the idea of a God "as I understood Him" seemed too limiting. Did people really believe a rock or a tree was their god, as I had been told?

I finally came to realize that it is exactly all any of us knows about God – the limitation is indeed our own understanding. We each have the freedom to trust the God of our own understanding and to understand that God according to our relationship experiences with Him. Those of us who have placed our full faith and trust in Jesus Christ know Him personally. Others know Him from a distance, or intellectually or historically. Just as you may know me as only a name on a page, others know me personally as a family member or friend. Your choice!

1 Corinthians 13:12 says, "Now we see through a glass, darkly [dimly, unclearly], but then face to face. Now I know in part, but then I shall know just as I also am known." And further, "When I was a child I understood as a child [immaturely, incompletely, imperfectly], but when I became a man, I put away childish things." My thoughts, feelings, and actions were those of a child. Now it is time for me to grow up in my thinking, feeling, and acting. It is a journey I am enjoying!

Some People Who Have Influenced My Life

Monte – my mentor; Pat – my sponsor

All my family who are addicted to drugs, alcohol, food, tobacco, money, shopping, work, or religion

The alcoholics, in long-term recovery, who patiently shared their experience, strength, and hope

My sweet mother, the godliest woman I have ever known; and my 5'6" dad, the biggest man I ever knew; my generous brother; my courageous gifted nieces; my amazing son and his beautiful wife along with my two smart and talented grandchildren

My family doctor; a nurse at a hospital in 1959; my counselors at the Nord Center; a doctor in Plano, TX who told me many years ago about the power of acceptance which I did not believe until now; a counselor in Allen, TX who took no fee for his year-long services attempting to save my second marriage.

AA and Al-Anon friends in Ohio, Texas, and Florida; my four BFF's: Betty, Brenda, Carol and Rosalee

A Virginia friend who believed in me; Facebook friends who encouraged me

The authors, poets, singers, composers, musicians, and artists whose work inspired or comforted me

Students of all ages; teachers, preachers, principals, and bosses; my friend DD who believed in my dream to start a school

15 DISTORTED THINKING PATTERNS

1. *Filtering = magnifies negative details; filters out positives*

This is the thinking pattern of the ultra-pessimist. He likes to focus on the negative details, and in particular, exaggerate them while ignoring any positive traits. The President may have done a dozen wonderful things to help his countrymen, but this person just sees his errors.

2. *Polarized thinking = black or white, all or nothing, right or wrong, good or bad, perfect or failure; no middle ground, no gray areas allowed*

More common than you might think, this polarized thinking pattern is one of the most frustrating because it is actually encouraged among certain groups. Refusing to consider that there might be a relationship-compromise between black and white called gray, or a political-compromise between red and blue called purple, they insist on being right and therefore, others must always be wrong. They are borderline suicidal because of their perfectionism; they are never able to truly BE perfect but cannot accept less in themselves or others.

3. *Over-generalizing* = *opinion based on a single piece of evidence*

This is the root cause of all bigotry and prejudice, but it goes farther and broader than that. It is the so-called eyewitness to an alleged crime who insists that the young man who walked down her street after running out of gas last week is indeed the one who broke into her garage. Or one unfortunate member of a family gets arrested, therefore it is evident that he comes from a "bad family."

4. *Mind reading* = *you "know" what a person's motives and feelings are; only God knows that*

This one is so insidious that it is difficult to give an example. These people pride themselves on having special insight, a gift they call it, which enables them to "know" things that others just cannot possibly know. The biblical gifts of knowledge, discernment, and wisdom can be misused this way. When pinned down to give some logical reasoning as to why they know what they think they know, these "gifted" people just insist that they know, that's all. A degree of stubbornness is required to read minds.

5. *Catastrophizing = expecting disaster; "what if" becomes an imminent tragedy; small problem magnified*

This is the man who gets the news that the washing machine quit working and keeps snowballing it until it's the end of the world.

6. *Personalizing = thinking the actions and words of others are a direct reaction to you*

A low self-image, lacking in proper self-esteem drives this distortion. Because these people often wait until something happens to "re-act" themselves, they think others do the same. Most of us are not that important in the world to have everything be about us anyways. Like the joke about the football players in a huddle. "Are they talking about me?" she wonders.

7. *Control fallacy = helpless victim VS being the one who caused others' pain; neither is true*

It is a mystery to me how the same person can act like he is the cause of all kinds of unfortunate circumstances, and yet at the same time, he bewails his own misery with no sense of accountability for causing it. This is a control freak run amuck for sure! He is so "powerful" he can cause misery on the world but cannot possibly be to blame for his own poor decisions which actually caused his own pain.

8. Fairness fallacy = resentful because you think you know what's fair and others don't

This indeed is a godlike creature. She is justice personified, having perfect judgment about what is and is not fair for everyone. Second graders suffer from this but most of them eventually grow up and learn that there is no such thing as genuine fairness on this planet.

9. Blaming = blaming others as the cause of your pain but, on the other hand, you take no responsibility for any pain anyone else suffers because of you

This one is similar to the control freak above with one exception: he has no accountability at all for any misery in the world. He did not cause his own pain; someone else is at fault. He did not cause any of your pain either. This person is truly stuck.

10. "Should" = ironclad rules cause you anger when others break them but you also feel very guilty when you break them, too

This is similar to the fairness fallacy. This person tries so hard to follow all the "rules of life," but never quite succeeds, feeling guilty all the time for his imperfection and subsequently pointing the finger at everyone else who also disobeys the "rules" in a subconscious effort to divert attention from his own flaws.

11. *Emotional reasoning = believing that feelings are truth; "what I feel I am"; feelings can be made up – acting*

Emotions can be faked; thus, the acting profession exists. My mind tells me "your mother is dead" and I begin to grieve as if it is true. I watch a movie and cry, or get angry, or become afraid. My emotions do not know the difference between fiction and reality. My mind needs to recognize the unreliability of feelings, and therefore learn to look at reality through logic and reason, and trust God through faith for other things that cannot be reasoned out logically.

12. *Fallacy of change = others will change to suit you if you pressure or manipulate them; it all depends on YOU*

This might be one of the most insidious distorted thinking patterns of all. It seems to be the root of some religious instruction. I was told that I could "change the world" if I prayed right, persuaded right, taught right, lived right, gave right ... the eternal fate of millions was on my shoulders. In relationships with men, I accepted men who "needed to change" many of their less-than-stellar character traits because I could love him enough to change him into the man he ought to be. And I felt guilty when no amount of loving persuasion changed him; in fact, he got worse. Pressure only solidifies a substance, but it takes millions of years, they say, to turn coal into diamonds!

13. *Global labeling = generalizes one or two qualities into a negative global judgment; basis of prejudice*

Similar to over-generalizing and black-and-white thinking, global labeling assigns the same negative traits to everyone in a group - the whole family, that entire race, everyone from New York – are all alike. Or on an individual basis, a person may have one or two negative traits, and therefore the conclusion is that he is personally ALL bad. NO ONE is ALL bad, not even a serial killer!

14. *Being right = feel you are always on trial to prove that your opinions or actions are correct; unthinkable to be wrong*

This distorted thinking pattern is evident in an argumentative person. He loves to argue about things that are completely subjective – his own opinions! But he goes further with it because he feels compelled to PROVE he is right – ALWAYS right! It would be unthinkable to actually BE wrong. He is like a man beating a dead horse – useless activity for both.

15. *Heaven's reward fallacy = expecting all your sacrifices and self-denial to pay off as if someone is keeping score; bitterness takes root when the rewards do not come*

This is the self-imposed martyr at her best. Self-denial, looking out for the best interests of others but not her own, sacrificing all for the greater good is fine except when there's an expectation of reward. If bad things happen instead, resentment and bitterness take over her life.

AAA to the Rescue!

I am a member of AAA Road Service. I call them when I have a flat tire or need to be towed if my car won't run. They come to the rescue, fix things and get me going on my way again.

The three A's from an Al-Anon slogan can do something similar.

The first A stands for Awareness. First I have to be aware that I have a flat. I can hear the funny noise, feel the bump bump bump of the car, but if I do not see it for what it is – a flat – I could continue to drive on it, ruining the tire for good. It cannot be fixed unless I am aware of it. I have to face the truth. If I imagine I need gas, stop at a gas station, and fill the tank, I will drive away with the same bump bump bump noise! A full tank of gas will not fix the problem. I have to see it in all its reality. It is what it is.

The second A stands for Acceptance. I have to accept the situation for what it is. It will not get fixed without acceptance. If I lie to myself about the true nature of the problem, it will never get fixed. I cannot keep telling myself I do not really have a flat, that the road is just bumpy. I have to accept the facts: I have a flat tire. It also requires that I accept who is responsible for fixing the problem. If it is my car and I am alone on the road, AAA is the one who will fix it because I have already paid for the service in advance [being proactive] and they have agreed to respond to my call for help. We have a contract in which we have agreed to be accountable to each other for it. I pay and they do the work. Good deal all around.

The third A stands for Action. Now, and only now, I am ready to do something productive and positive. Now, and only now, I am ready to do what is really needed, not what I imagined. I am ready to be proactive and take appropriate action, not impulsively reacting, only to shoot first and ask questions later. Now my action will be appropriate, and the end result will be satisfying. I make the phone call to AAA and wait patiently for the results.

In my personal life, I often got these three confused and in the wrong order. I saw there was a problem which needed attention, and assuming [bad idea!] I was the one who could, should, and would solve the problem, I took action. I did not stop to consider if it was my husband's responsibility to take action. He often responded with, "I don't know what to do; I don't have any answers." He rolled the problem and the accountability for the outcome onto my shoulders. It was his problem to gain awareness, his problem to accept, and his problem to fix.

When all is said and done, however, I still must finish with Acceptance. Accept the results of your actions or the results of another's actions. Without acceptance, there can be no serenity.

Acceptance Is the Key to Serenity

Acceptance used to be my most hated word. I saw it as weakness or mediocrity. I heard, "Oh well, I guess I just have to accept this situation," and I said, "Oh, no I don't! I am a doer, not just a dreamer!"

I was so wrong.

Acceptance really is the magic key which unlocks serenity any time and any place I need it. Any situation, however unpleasant, unwanted, uncomfortable can be transformed into peacefulness of my spirit with acceptance. I didn't say the situation changed. It might still be just as unpleasant, unwanted, and uncomfortable as ever, but I have been changed. I have been transformed by a change in my thinking, in my attitude. I can now handle the situation gracefully, calmly, and peacefully.

Romans chapter 12 says to "... be transformed by renewing your mind ..." Change your thinking patterns; choose what you think about and how you think about it. One slogan says, "Think about what you're thinking about." That means to give serious consideration to how you think and what you are thinking. When I choose to accept the reality of a situation, I can have serenity immediately. I do not have to wait for everything and everyone else to get better!

I am empowered by the serenity that settles into my soul so that I can face whatever is coming at me; I can face whatever criticism, whatever bad news, whatever bad weather, whatever financial upsets. Just name it and acceptance will bring me "peace which passes all understanding." I can then act if necessary, but my actions will be more productive because I have changed my attitude. As long as I am mentally fighting, resisting what is real, I can do little to solve it.

Jesus prayed His most difficult prayer - for acceptance - in the Garden before His arrest. He prayed, "God, not my will, but your will be done." That's the highest level of acceptance. Do I really think I – a mere mortal – can achieve peace in any other way?

We have been instructed since childhood to end our prayers with "in the name of Jesus, amen." What does that really mean? It means, in my opinion, that we are asking according to God's will. Jesus's name is flawless; it is the best. It stands for perfection, for the truth. If I ask for anything according to "flawless, perfection" - the name of Jesus - it must be within the boundaries of His will. It must also be motivated by perfect love ... for God, for myself and for others.

Of course God will not reply positively to any request that violates His own plan for our ultimate good. As a human parent, I admit I sometimes said, "Okay, you have my permission, reluctantly." I believed it wasn't best for my child, but either I said yes and set some boundaries to protect him, or he would do it anyway, violating my will and possibly endangering himself.

Asking God for what we need in faith believing He will do it is only possible if we ask in His name – according to God's will. Unlike us, as imperfect parents, God's actions ARE perfect, always in our best interests. We can trust Him to allow nothing that will not ultimately result in our good. Romans 8:28 says it so well – God is working all things together for our good. Everything that happens is not good in itself, but when we acknowledge Him in all our ways – see it from HIS perspective - HE works things out for our benefit.

Pain is inevitable in life; suffering is optional. Problems are a given in life; stress is optional. Stress is such a popular word these days, but it is really a revealing word. When we say we are stressed out, we are telling everyone that we have problems and pain for which we do not have adequate coping skills.

EVERYONE has problems and pain at some time in life. Many people have far more serious pain and far worse problems than I have, but many of them have more peace.

Why is it that some people appear to suffer less, cope better, and generally be happier in spite of their pain?

The secret is just their ability to think differently about it – they have rejected stress and suffering in exchange for simplicity and serenity.

Acceptance begins with humility and gratitude. I must see the truth, the reality of my circumstances without a "spoiled child entitlement" attitude. "Why me?" is fine to ask God when we are trying to cope, but if we stay there constantly whining "why me, why me, why me" it is obvious that we have little humility and even less gratitude.

Why NOT me? Who am I to deserve better than others? Who am I to decide that God has made some kind of mistake? Acceptance says I agree with God that this situation, this circumstance, this person, this place, this "problem" is exactly what God has either allowed in my life or has placed there on purpose – for HIS purpose – to shape my character more into conformity with His.

On the other hand, perhaps I would discover, if the truth were faced squarely, that the pain was caused by my own distorted thinking in the first place and not God's will at all. Acceptance begins with the truth encased in humility and gratitude. Pride insists on its own way; a lack of gratitude stems from that pride as well.

Anger, loneliness, fear, worry, resentment, bitterness, envy, jealousy, hurtful gossip and all other negative attitudes have at their root an entitled ungrateful spirit.

I am angry because I expected something I did not get or got something I did not want. MY WAY!

I am lonely because I expected someone to be with me who doesn't want to be here. MY WAY!

I am fearful or worried because I cannot find the courage to trust my Higher Power with the situation or problem. MY WAY!

I am resentful or bitter, envious or jealous because someone got something I thought I deserved but I did not get. MY WAY!

I engage in hurtful jealous gossip because I secretly want to diminish the status of someone who got what I wanted. MY WAY!

All these attitudes are rooted in a lack of humility – arrogant pride – and a lack of gratitude. When I humbly admit that I deserve nothing and gratefully accept and thank God for what I do have, I am on the way to serenity – a peace which cannot be understood, as the Bible says, gratefully trusting God, accepting His will in all things.

I want to be more like the God of my understanding – Jesus Christ – who prayed his most fervent and, I dare say, most difficult prayer for acceptance. Since he had laid aside most of his deity to humble himself and come to earth as a mere human, he demonstrated for us the pathway to peace at his most difficult moment in human flesh – his impending death.

He showed humility, acceptance, forgiveness, and compassion as he died – FOR US! Could I not LIVE –

happily – in the same way showing humility, acceptance, forgiveness, and compassion?

Addicted to Alcoholic Men!

Loving an alcoholic is next to impossible for me, but falling in love with one is what I do best! I really want to be in a mutually satisfying relationship with a sane mature man, but it has not happened for me. I am drawn to alcoholic men like a moth to a flame. It seems to be my nature. Why? I have no idea, but this book is a collection of the essays I have written trying to find my own peace – my serenity – while loving these alcoholics.

If you are expecting scintillating stories of the alcoholics' cruelties, you may be disappointed. I really do love alcoholics, and they deserve to be respected as members of the human family and God's creation. My dilemma is that it has often hurt me to love an alcoholic. They were "AAA men" – angry, abusive, alcoholics.

The irony is that it has been those very same men [and women] who have tried to help ME! One I loved finally convinced me to go to Al-Anon meetings. One I loved tried to teach me some of the AA principles earlier in my life. One by his example of recovery has inspired me to seek my own recovery. One helped me get away from an abusive husband; I went back to him anyways. One helped me get through a break-up with another alcoholic. One is even my greatest encourager to publish this book! I am surrounded by alcoholic men and women whom I have loved and who have loved me!

I was married to an active alcoholic for only a short time; I have been "sick" for most of my life. I keep getting into relationships with alcoholics, unwittingly. These men are as different as could be. The one constant in all these relationships is ME! I am the determining factor; something in ME is attracted to this disease. I am on a quest to discover what that is. Perhaps, as one alcoholic friend suggested, I am sicker than all of them!

I am devastated by the pain I have experienced, but it is my own fault. I believed their promises, knowing in my heart these men cannot make commitments, cannot keep promises as much as they may want to. One alcoholic promised me an inheritance of hundreds of thousands of dollars which I had done nothing to deserve. Never have I gotten it twenty years after his death. Another promised me fidelity – I got anything but fidelity. One promised me he would tell me the truth and I could trust him not to hurt me. He toyed with my heart, I got caught up in his fantasies, and it hurt me deeply.

One alcoholic actually told me a great truth, "All alcoholics are con men." In my crazy mind, I thought, "Yes, they are ... except for you!"

I am apparently under a spell, [ha!] perhaps even a curse, which compels me to love them without boundaries. That may sound a little like martyrdom, but it isn't. I am not really a victim except of my own ignorance and naiveté. I DID IT TO MYSELF!

I have learned more from my relationships with alcoholics than I have from relationships with healthy people. However, living with an alcoholic is an education and a challenge, and more power to all the spouses, siblings and children who must do so. Al-Anon is a good place to get loving support.

As a result of living with and loving alcoholics, I have developed a "sickness" too, but I don't drink. It is a family disease, not so much inherited genetically as passed down through a lifestyle of distorted thinking. Yes, there is scientific evidence that some people may be genetically predisposed to becoming alcoholics. The tricky thing is that NOT drinking or drugging does not mean one is not an alcoholic! Likewise, drinking does not automatically make one an alcoholic!

The disease is "between the ears" and must be treated "between the ears." The symptoms of drinking, drugging, smoking, overeating, gambling, compulsive shopping, or even over-working may be eliminated, but the disease is still as actively destructive as ever "between the ears" and evidenced in all their relationships.

It is a disease of EXTREMES! Alcoholics are among the smartest, most productive, successful people in the world. The drunk in the gutter is no different from the executive in the boardroom except in geography and economics. One of the biggest lies an alcoholic has to overcome is the one which says, "I can't be an alcoholic because I am financially successful." The alcoholics I have loved are all financially well off, successful in the community, and well-liked.

They just can't seem to have long-term, mutually satisfying relationships with one woman. In my experience, they are fishermen – they pursue the catch with specially chosen lures and lines, and then, just when the fish has been caught and lies squirming and gasping for breath, he throws her back in only to be caught again by another fisherman. They are "collectors of women." They crave an intimate relationship with one woman, but when she falls in love with him, he pushes her away or keeps her at arm's length. They have trouble allowing someone to really love them. Their egos are enormous, hence the difficulty with humility. Ironically, they also suffer from feelings of low self-worth. They generate a brand of humility when they say in a meeting, "Hi, my name is _____ and I am an alcoholic," but it can almost become a thoughtless routine thing, much like church-goers mumbling recitations!

The mistake I believe most of us make in trying to "diagnose" alcoholism is that we only look at external behaviors instead of looking for the distorted thinking patterns which motivated the behavior.

Identifying an alcoholic is made more difficult by the fact that some respected institutions and organizations are built on distorted thinking. They constantly vilify their members with guilt and condemnation for having the disease of alcoholism while declaring they have the cure. This encourages the alcoholic to cover up his illness and delay seeking recovery because of the guilt. No one is to blame for the drinking except the alcoholic, that is clear, but why do some institutions put up such roadblocks to recovery while claiming to have the cure?

Sobriety does NOT indicate the absence of alcoholism! There are "dry alcoholics" who have never touched a drop. They may exhibit symptoms by eating obsessively, by gambling compulsively, by chain smoking, by over-working, by excessive shopping or hoarding. "Alcoholism" is defined by thinking patterns which express themselves in EXTREMES, in obsessive compulsive behaviors.

To complicate matters more, people with clinical OCD are not necessarily alcoholics. People who manage to live within socially acceptable norms may still be alcoholics, and people who live outside the social norms may not be alcoholics. It is difficult to identify alcoholism!

Al-Anon exists simply for anyone who has been affected by a loved one's drinking. It does not attempt to cure alcoholism. However, to understand all this better and to decide if a 12-step program might be right for you, the best questions to ask yourself about the alcoholic are the following:

> What "inspires" him to drink? [or smoke, eat, buy, work, gamble]
> When does he choose to drink? [or smoke, eat, buy, work, gamble]
> With whom, where, or how does he drink? [or smoke, eat, buy, work, gamble]

THE most important question is "Does any of this bother me?"

The answers to these questions may help ... a little. Even the alcoholic does not know the answers for sure. He is driven to drink by a force he cannot control and does not understand. Perhaps that is the answer to why I am attracted to them. It is a force I cannot control and certainly do not comprehend.

I need to remember that these are imperfect human beings with a disease they cannot cure. I am also an imperfect human being with a similar incurable disease. We are ALL broken; most know it; some do not; few are willing to admit it.

Expectations are premeditated resentments. An alcoholic can only love you in his limited way. Accept that or leave him alone. Your love hungry heart will never be satisfied. You will NEVER be able to love him enough to change him. Only God can do that.

Advice and . . . Confusion!

Unwanted advice can do a great deal of harm.

Unwanted, unsolicited advice bombarded me when I went through a divorce after thirty years of marriage. I had no job, but I was advised that I MUST keep the house. Then I was advised that I MUST NOT keep the house. I was told to do a number of frankly crazy things. It took all the energy I had to make decisions that were in my own best interest. I am sure that if I had listened to some of them, I would still be in court, owing many more thousands of dollars to my lawyer, and ready for desperate measures. If it had not been for Al-Anon and AA, loyal family and true friends, I would not have survived it. I am certain.

My old friend Job had three friends who meant well and probably cared for him. They were there, weren't they? But they didn't help at all. They talked and talked, but none of the talk helped. Talk doesn't help.

Saying, "If I were you ..." is stupid. You are NOT me! You have not lived my life, had my experiences, my education – formal or otherwise – and you do not have a clue about what GOD thinks is best and right for ME. And by the way, if you were me, you would do exactly what I did ... because that's what I'd do if I were you being me!

Then what empowers individuals to make decisions which are in their own best interests? Acceptance, encouragement, and confidence boosters like the following have always helped me:

"You're smart. I know you will make the right decision."

"Meditate, ask God for guidance, listen for an answer, believe it, then get up and go do it."

"Read the Bible or good literature on the topic which perplexes you."

"Follow YOUR standards. Stop considering what others think. Do what's best for YOU."

"Do the next right thing."

"Listen to the experience, strength, and hope of those who have walked the same valley. They might know a safer passage through it."

Notice nobody told me exactly WHAT to do or WHAT to think; they just empowered me with confidence in myself and faith in my Higher Power.

I believe our schools and even our churches are doing us a terrible disservice by teaching WHAT to think instead of teaching HOW to think! That is called indoctrination and brain-washing, the ultimate control-freak behavior.

Let's stop being controllers and start being "empower-ers."

"Are You Lonesome Tonight?"

Loneliness can be a natural by-product of the simple, serene life I have chosen to live – minding my own business, not expecting anyone else to make me happy, taking care of myself, and living one day at a time.

HALT tells me to watch out for being hungry, angry, lonely or tired. For me, I have discovered that they seem to come in the following pairs:

"tired - hungry"

"tired - lonely"

"angry - hungry"

"lonely - hungry"

I am rarely "angry – tired" or "angry – lonely" any more. Odd pairing, I guess, but it has been the pattern in my life. When I am angry, I usually have taken it out on myself by over-eating. Notice I am frequently hungry when I am tired or angry or lonely! Why do I punish myself when I am really angry at someone else or some circumstance or situation I cannot control? Perhaps it is because expressions of anger were not allowed in my upbringing. Eating could be done in private, and since everyone has to eat to survive, I could simply stuff my angry feelings down my throat with a Twinkie or a bag of chips.

Feeling lonely is entirely my problem to solve. All I have to do is make a phone call to a friend, plan an outing, do some project or chore on my own "To Do List," connect with friends through social media, take a walk at the park, or even go visit an elderly friend in a nursing home. I have options! I do not have to live with those lonely feelings. Feeling lonely and doing nothing to change it comes from feeling like a helpless victim or a child and therefore a desire for pity. I must reject both self-pity and loneliness.

When I choose to be alone, I must remember I am not choosing to be lonely. Big difference! Loneliness is a feeling of isolation, deprivation, even rejection. Isolation can be remedied by calling someone or getting together with a friend. Feeling deprived has at its root an ungrateful attitude – it seems to say I have missed out, been overlooked, been cheated, or simply not received something I think I deserve.

Rejection runs deeper. Perhaps in the past when I have been lonely I have reached out to spend time with a friend and been told "no." But feelings of rejection are just that – feelings, and feelings can be liars. Feelings can change; they are temporary. Feelings are RE-actions to thoughts or actions; feelings must not be allowed to take control. Perhaps the friend just had no desire to do the activity. Perhaps it had nothing to do with me at all. Perhaps there was no personal rejection involved.

Telling someone else that "I am lonely" is often an attempt at manipulation; I want them to fix my loneliness. It says, "Do something! Make me not feel lonely anymore!" But it is a helpless feeling to hear those words from someone I love. I just cannot fix it for them. And frankly, I often recoil from those words; it makes me uncomfortable. I simply cannot be held accountable for their loneliness.

On the other hand, having a friend with whom I can be honest and say "I am feeling lonely" can help IF that friend is honest enough not to enable the loneliness. I have learned that being lonely or not and being alone or not are both choices I can make. As my dear Dr. O said, I can be alone and miserable or alone and happy, with someone and miserable or with someone and happy. All four are separate choices – happy, miserable, alone or with someone!

I have been lonely in the presence of another person or in a large crowd. I have felt content and peaceful when alone. My serenity does not depend on other people being present or absent. My serenity depends on my attitude at the moment. I choose first to be at peace with God and myself; therefore, I will be more at peace with or without the company of friends.

"As a man thinks, so is he."

"All We Have to Fear is Fear Itself"

Winston Churchill

Fear has been an ally in my unwitting effort to underachieve! I have called upon my fear instead of my faith on many occasions. In fact, my fear and my fat have been double allies – if I wasn't really afraid to do it, I used my shameful excess weight as a reason to hide in the shadows, afraid of criticism. Courage, on the other hand, is doing what must be done and facing the consequences, whatever they may be.

I used to live in fear of ...
People in general = a group called "they"
Technology and machines
Being judged wrongly
Being truly nuts
Large crowds
Scary movies and books
Small spaces

Not living up to expectations
Being beheaded
Guns, knives and other lethal weapons
The future
Being seen as incompetent or stupid
Murder
Being fired
Spiders and centipedes
Going to jail
Snakes
Falling down in public as an old lady
Mice
Losing a body part or one of my senses
Roaches
Losing control of my bodily functions in public
Big dogs
Getting lost in a large city
Losing my purse
Missing the school bus
Being naked in public
Being truly homeless living under a bridge
Being rejected
Being made fun of behind my back
Being disliked
Having friends who are disloyal
Bloody injuries
Hospitals, doctors' offices, all medical procedures
Breaking a bone

Failing in a desperate attempt to kill myself!

What a list, huh? It is almost laughable except for how seriously fearful I was!

Now I have peace, in spite of my fears. My fears draw me nearer to my God, and that makes my fear a good thing. When I stand up and face my fears head on, I am exercising my faith in my God and I am agreeing with Him about His word which says, "I can do all things through Christ Who strengthens me." In addition, I am looking in the mirror and saying "I CAN DO THIS," thus encouraging myself. The Bible says that David "encouraged himself." I can encourage myself, too! 365 times the Word of God says, "Fear not!" That's one for every day of the year!

Is my list of fears still that long? Yes and no, but I realize that most of my fears will probably never happen so why allow any of those things to control me now? Those that do confront me will be met with courage, faith in God, and reasonable caution.

Some of the fears on my list are really out of my control completely because they have to do with other people's opinions or behavior. Those are none of my business whatsoever.

Some of the fears on my list are unavoidable such as going to the doctor or hospital, but with new methods of thinking, feeling and behaving through my twelve step program, I can actually embrace them – with courage, faith in God who loves me and has only my best interests at heart, and reasonable caution.

Some of my fears can be handled with the attitude that I can only do the best I can do, and when I mess up, I will accept it. I will not beat myself up over it, realizing that everyone makes mistakes. I am no better than others. I will be accountable and 'fess up if I mess up. Then I will try to do better next time. That's really all I can do.

Some of my fears can be met simply with a sense of humor. So what if I fall down on a public street? Someone will probably help me get up, and I can laugh it off demonstrating true grace and poise.

Fear is an insidious creature with no courage because, when confronted, fear scurries away. What a coward! As the Cowardly Lion said in The Wizard of Oz, "Put 'em uuuuuppp!"

Can You Validate?

Have you ever gone to an important meeting in a high rise building that has its own multi-level parking facility? If you have business in their building, you may avoid the parking charge by having your ticket validated, or stamped, in the office where you had your meeting. It feels good to walk to your car, knowing you do not have to pay the high price of parking. Validation is a very good thing!

There is a saying I found somewhere, "Come live in my heart and pay no rent." I love that. Come park in my garage and pay no rent because I have acknowledged you as having business with me. Come live in my heart – let me love you – and it will cost you nothing.

I am well-loved by several people; I have four loyal friends who have been there for me since childhood. But when it comes to the men in my life – grandfathers, father, brother, uncles, cousins, husbands, a son and grandson – I still feel that I must "pay a price" to deserve their love. It is clearly MY problem, not theirs. I imagine they will not love me on my own merits; I have to DO something or BE something – to suit them – before I will really have their love. For the most part, I don't feel that way about the women in my life – my mother, daughter-in-law, granddaughter, aunts, nieces, cousins, and friends. For some reason, I feel validated, assured that their love is freely given with no expectation of "payment."

Validation can be used as a legal term referring to the confirmation of truth. Confirmation is sometimes a religious term referring to the ceremony of validating the certainty of one's faith. When we use it in regard to relationships, it refers more to the assertion that one is a worthy human being, deserving of love and appreciation, acknowledgment that you "belong."

Both times I got married, I requested that this Bible passage from the book of Ruth be included in the ceremony: "Entreat me not to leave thee nor to return from following after thee, for where thou goest, I will go ..." To me it indicates the essence of an intimate relationship. But it also says something about me that I wanted it included both times. Both husbands, in their anger, would often scream at me to leave: "Get out!" This was such a horrible feeling of rejection I cannot describe it in words. I had pledged myself each time, believing, with all my heart that MY devotion was real, genuine, true, and yet, it never seemed to be enough.

I always felt that I did not have my sweet dad's approval, his validation. He confirmed that in my mind on his death bed when his last words to me were, "I guess I will never see you skinny." I thought, yes you did see me at a normal size, but it was still not good enough. I know he loved me, but I felt he never quite approved of me. I felt I had to pay to live in his heart – and he died before I could pay my debt by getting skinny. I wonder, laughingly now, how he would have decided if I was skinny enough? A dress size, a weight, my body mass index number, or a doctor's diagnosis of "skinny"? A co-worker friend suggested that perhaps he was actually expressing his own regret that he would not be here to see my certain success! What a blessing to think of it that way!

Our loved ones, who drink or do drugs or have any other addiction over which they are powerless, desperately need our validation. This is a complicated problem. We don't like their behavior of drinking, but we love them. It is hard to separate the person from the action. In Al-Anon we call it "detachment with love." The alcoholic needs validation as much as anyone – perhaps more. They need to know they can live in our hearts without payment. They have enough guilt and inner turmoil without the added suffering of our rejection. On the other hand, we have the right to set boundaries for how they treat us.

I remember the power my own words had on a young student in my fifth grade class. She was taller than all the other kids, her mousy brown hair hung in her face, and she walked kind of stooped over, I assumed, both because she was getting breasts and because she was so tall. As she slumped along in line from recess one afternoon, I commented, "Saundra, you know, models are always tall women; you should pull back your shoulders, hold your head up high, and be proud of your body." Seven years later, as I cleaned up my classroom on the last day of school, her mother visited me. She came to show me Saundra's modeling portfolio! Words are powerful.

Come . . . live in my heart . . . and pay no rent. My love is free. You do not need to earn it. You are good enough for me to love just as you are ... no payment required! I am glad God required no payment before He chose to love me. The Bible says, "While you were still imperfect, Christ died for you." That's the kind of love I want. That's the kind of love I want to give.

The reality, however, is that, if you want to have an intimate personal relationship with me, I have boundaries and there will be some mutual accountability agreed upon between us. I will love you unconditionally, but ... I cannot be anyone's doormat again. I cannot live with everyone I love. As Sol Gordon, Ph.D. said in his book, <u>Why Love Is Not Enough,</u> love alone is not a good enough reason to get married or live with someone. I am free and willing to love all of mankind, allowing them to be exactly who they are without the necessity of change for my sake, but if another human being wants to live in my house, we gotta talk!

Care and Concern - or Control and Codependent?

My mother is a saint, honest to God, right up there with Mother Teresa, just waiting for her crown to make it official. She really is the godliest woman I have ever known, bar none. But ... (you knew there was a but coming!)

She apparently expresses her love for others – her love language, if you will – by doing good deeds for them and buying gifts. She seems to have a bit of all five love languages, according to Dr. Chapman's book of the same title. She also seems to show evidence of all nine "fruit of the spirit" from Galatians in the Bible, the list which most believers aspire to develop more and more in our lives.

Personally, I am lacking in more than one of these fruit, and I fear some have even rotted a bit. And my love languages? Time, talk, and touch in that order, please. I do not FEEL as loved by receiving gifts or having someone wait on me hand and foot as I do just by their spending time with me, talking to me in positive ways, and holding my hand or giving me a hug. I greatly appreciate everything others have given me and done for me, but ...

I guess gifts and good deeds from my husband have too often felt like manipulation or even control measures TO ME, while time is a commodity which cannot be replaced once it is spent. Money can be accumulated again. Time cannot. I know, talk is cheap, but the kind of talk I appreciate is meaningful, encouraging positive communication, not unwanted advice, gossip, or just small talk. I like "big talk" instead. I enjoy interesting conversation about history, religion, politics, issues, art, music, and ideas with people who are not argumentative or know-it-alls, but people who have an open mind and really want to exchange ideas and feelings, not lecture me!

I care about people, really I do. I have real physical "sympathy pains" when people get hurt, but if you are broken or bleeding, I am not the one you want nearby. I do not have an ounce of nursing skill in my body. Yes, I managed to raise a son without injury or serious illness, and I taught elementary school for over thirty years with no serious incidents. However, I am most likely to cry, run for help, and cry some more, maybe do some hand-wringing or (when I was younger) some jumping up and down accompanied by more tears. I care about people, really I do. (Here comes another but ...)

I have a motto I live by in all my relationships, whether children [not infants] or adults, men or women, sick or well, smart or not so. "Don't do anything for them that they CAN do for themselves." They may not CHOOSE to do it for themselves, and that's OK with me. They may not do it as WELL as I could have, and that's OK too. I believe it is an insult to an adult when another adult treats her like a helpless baby.

My last husband [I am apparently collecting them?] used to say to me that I called him stupid. I simply do not call people names, but now I realize that when I did things he COULD do, even if I could do them "better" - more quickly, more efficiently, more attractively, more anything – I was treating him as if he were stupid. Truthfully, I DID think I could do some things better, but he could also definitely do some things better than I could. I stepped over certain boundaries – got into areas which were not my business – when I did for him what he should and could have done for himself. Oops.

My loving mother laid out my dad's clothes for him, polished his shoes, controlled his diabetic diet [he still sneaked bad food], ironed everything including his socks and underwear, and in every way that a "good" wife should, she took care of him. He loved it, but if she had died first, I would have pitied his next wife! I don't believe in doing things for people when they can do them on their own. I don't believe in one adult in a household being the other adult's servant. I think that was outlawed in 1863 when slavery was abolished, right?

My mother was a stay-at-home mom who almost never worked outside the home. She did domestic chores most of the time when she did have outside jobs. My dad went to work every day faithfully and was a good provider. He gave my mom his paycheck every two weeks, and she managed the money quite well. He took care of the maintenance of the house, yard, garden, and the cars. He helped with the inside work when he retired, and finally he could and would do anything she could do around the house – the laundry, cooking, dish-washing, vacuuming, dusting, window-washing – you name it. They had a good agreement about division of labor.

The problem, in my view, was that she did things for my dad, a grown man, and for my brother and me as we grew up, that we could and should have done for ourselves. Her motives were good. I didn't choose my own clothes, do my own hair, or make many decisions for myself until I was in junior high. And then it was difficult to wrest control of my own body and my own life out of her hands. The only two areas in which I knew I had complete control were my weight and my intellect. I could "control" my own weight by sneaking food and eating as I pleased, and I could get good grades on my own. I didn't need any help or permission to do either one. Fortunately I chose to do well on grades, but unfortunately my weight was tied to out-of-control emotions and low self-esteem.

People who express love by doing good deeds have a more difficult time letting their alcoholic take responsibility for themselves than perhaps people with one of the other love languages do. It is so hard to stand by and "let" them do a poor job of taking care of themselves.

If you want to help others, help them in ways that do not wound their self-esteem. Go shopping together and give her the money, discreetly, for payment just before you reach the check-out. Give a gift card for a specific store – groceries, gas, fast food, haircuts, dollar stores, laundry and dry cleaning – if you want to be sure it goes for essentials. Then go with him to buy the items he needs. [Remember grocery stores and gas stations sometimes sell alcohol.] But be discreet about the transaction between you.

Gift-giving and money-giving can be a wonderful expression of love. In my experience, it has not always been so wonderful to be on the receiving end. I have done both, and believe me it is "more blessed to give than to receive." One of the things with the most strings attached can be material gifts and money.

My second motto is this: "Anything given away is no longer yours to control." If I give an expensive gift to a friend and he takes it outside, smashes it, and scatters the pieces all over the street, it is none of my business. He may be arrested for littering, and I will think twice before buying him another expensive gift he obviously dislikes, but what he does with that item is his business. It became his when I gave it to him!

Giving money should be done judiciously when it involves an addict, but consider your giving style. Are you trying to avoid encouraging an addiction, or are you trying to control the addict with that gift of money? If you want to help keep him from starving on the street, suggest a good shelter and then give your donation of food, money, or blankets to the shelter which can help everyone. The shelter will appreciate it, you can keep your serenity, and the alcoholic is not enabled by your kindness. Even taking him to the shelter, if he needs transportation, is within the boundaries of wise caring.

Keeping in mind "not to do for anyone anything they can do for themselves," and remembering that "anything given away is no longer yours to control" will help you retain your serenity and still show loving, caring concern for others.

Alcoholics, children, the elderly, and the handicapped need to feel empowered, to feel capable and to feel as self-sufficient as everyone else. Love them enough to let them do everything they can!

Communicating Doesn't Mean Talking It to Death

I'm a talker. I love to talk.

I didn't talk much until sixth grade. I was unleashed that year, and my wonderful teacher, Mrs. Pickworth, must have been frustrated by it. She knew I had a reputation for being a "quiet studious" child, so my chattering must have perplexed her; she moved me all over the room to find a place where I would be less tempted. She finally found it – at the end of the far right side row with no one behind, no one to the right, an empty desk to the left of me, a boy who would not talk to anyone in front of me, and a boy in front of the empty desk who I thought was a criminal and scared me to death. Perfect!

I am so grateful that she handled it that way. I was a good student, I loved to learn, and my chatter was usually commentary about the lesson she was teaching. She did not treat me like a bad kid as some might have. She adjusted, not even expecting or requiring me to change; she didn't even punish me. I was still very shy in front of the whole class, so I am sure she understood how devastating it would have been for me to be branded "bad" for talking.

I wasn't learning how to communicate, however. Communication is not talk. Conversation is not necessarily communication, just as sex isn't always "making love." By the way, intercourse actually first meant verbal communication! Interesting how a word that used to mean genuine communion on two levels now just means sex.

The word communication has the root word "commune" which signifies "sharing in common;" the word communion has the same root as the word "common". It is about commonality, not differences! It is intimate. Arguing and debating are not real communication. We communicate when we share common ideas, common feelings, common activities, common beliefs, or common sensory awareness. A barrage of words aimed at each other is not communication.

But what if we disagree? Real communication, communion, involves giving and receiving something. It means I receive you, your words, your ideas behind them, and I accept them at face value. I don't have to agree, but perhaps I can find in some part of it a way to understand better who you are. Communication does not mean that I listen and try to convince you to agree with my ideas; it does mean that I remain open-minded and accepting of your ideas and feelings. We then share something in common. Communication happens best with adults who are "equals," other adults with whom you do not feel "less than" in any way, nor do they feel "less than" you in any way. Otherwise you are not communicating, someone is just lecturing!

Words are powerful, but too often words are used as a way of beating others up. The old schoolyard taunt, "Sticks and stones may break my bones but words can never hurt me" is just not true in human experience, especially in mine. The bruises of sticks and stones heal rapidly, but the scars from a word-beating may go so deep, the victim may never recognize the source of his pain and continue to suffer.

My husband of thirty years did not communicate on any level. He sometimes talked, sometimes listened, and often just heard me with his physical ears. We had no "communion." Oh, we had a few interests in common.

We both enjoyed the Christmas movies on TV every season, but we just sat in the same room and watched them. When he talked to me, he either just told stories or he said basically the same things over and over – clichés - canned statements he picked up from someone else, or else he tried to "indoctrinate" me – force me to agree with his political opinions. Share his heart, his real heart? I never really knew the man, and sadly, I doubt that he knew himself. I am certain he didn't really know me.

Communication is both giving and receiving – sharing. It involves commonality, and that requires three things: understanding, acceptance, and meekness.

I think meekness, one of the nine most desirable fruit of the spirit named in the Bible, is a highly misunderstood word. A meek person, in my experience, is a confident, humble but teachable person, one with an open mind and a receptive heart. It requires humility plus inner strength, but not passivity. Meekness builds on the foundation of acceptance and patience. A meek person is submissive to authority or to anyone else, with confidence in himself, while maintaining his own integrity. Meekness, I define as confidence with open-minded humility, is an important prerequisite for genuine communication.

The dictionary says meek can mean "spineless," but why was Jesus called meek when He was enormously brave and strong? He knew exactly who He was and what His mission was. He was anything but spineless. Jesus was a "real" man. He called a spade a spade – He called the self-righteous religious leaders "snakes" and "hypocrites" and "whitewashed tombs." A spineless man would not do anything that risky! He was accepting and kind toward outcast sinners who were condemned by those same religious leaders, while he never approved of their behavior; He simply loved them, which in turn empowered them to change.

Did you get that? His love and acceptance empowered them to change! Condemnation, comparison, guilt-tripping, fear-mongering, and criticism do not inspire change; quite the opposite – they encourage rebellion, lying, excuse-making, self-hatred, and spitefulness. I used to "cut off my nose to spite my face" in response to those same tactics.

Discussions meant to "solve problems" can be very sticky, indeed. Between a husband and wife, things need to be discussed. I share my thoughts, opinions, and ideas about the issue; he shares his. We see if there is any common ground. If there is, we have a chance of reaching a compromise IF EACH of us is willing to give a little on our own ideas. If there is no common ground, God designed the concept of submission as a mean for handling power struggles. If an impasse occurs, one person MUST give in to the other person in order for there to be a decision made, to have progress. The natural outcome of pulling a rope at both ends only results in one person with rope burns dragging the other one into the mud!

Submission has been given a bad connotation by power-hungry, domineering, dictatorial, control freak men. In my experience, being in a relationship with a man like that inspires in me several responses but never submission. True biblical submission involves first, two people who see each other as respected equals; there are no little power games going on between them. One AA friend of mine related how he and his first wife had a silent war about the toilet paper – one wanted it coming off the roll over the top, and the other wanted it to come off the roll from underneath. They each changed the roll every time they went into the bathroom, which fueled their battles over everything else. They were equal all right – equal combatants!

Secondly, each is genuinely willing to accept and understand the other. If I have no sense of meekness, no willingness to truly see his point of view, the discussion is useless. There has to be this willingness on both parts, or here the communication ends. Words have emotional energy; be sure it is positive, constructive energy born of meekness and acceptance.

Thirdly, and most importantly, both must understand priorities - the principle of "how important is it" and value their relationship over anything else. No decision, about the things husbands and wives must decide together, is important enough to divide them. On their wedding day, I advised my son and daughter-in-law never to allow anything or anyone to separate them. There was a reason.

I remembered an embarrassing incident between my son's dad and me. He wanted to buy a red truck, but I didn't like red trucks. We got a divorce – not about the truck – but guess what? He bought a red truck. The real surprise is that I later bought a red vehicle myself. My tastes changed! I now call all these power struggles "red truck issues." How important was it? It was definitely not enough to argue about. And while the red truck issue was not what caused the divorce, the power struggle was a big part of it.

I have learned in my experience, to paraphrase what others say to me in an attempt to understand them. I have sometimes been surprised that my paraphrase – my understanding – was incorrect. Before I give my response, I try to say something like, "Correct me if I am wrong, but did you say ...?" You too might be surprised that what you heard was not their intended meaning.

Try to use "I statements" instead of accusing terms like "you did this and you did that." Saying "I feel this way when this happens" is indisputable. It is a statement of truth that belongs to you – your own feelings. "You" statements are accusations, and believe me, all the other person wants to do is to defend himself. In my experience, if I wanted real communication – including acceptance and understanding – I needed to speak with meekness.

Jesus was the best example of communication. Reading carefully the story of the woman at the well, you will see that He did not make accusations, simply statements of fact. She had a meek attitude – an open-minded, learner attitude – and she listened. We know she was meek because she did not deny or defend herself; she agreed that indeed she had had five husbands and was now living with a man, unmarried. There was no exchange of condemnation and defense – there was real communication. The result was that she became a believer and immediately "carried the message to others."

If you want to communicate, call his name often as you talk; it may seem simple, but it makes a world of difference. From the first day you ever recognized your own name, it has been your identity. Every time you hear it spoken by the one you love, it personalizes the conversation making it more intimately just between you. Children in school will act up badly just to hear their names called, research and my experience have shown.

Look her in the eye when she talks; do nothing else; don't multi-task when you are having a conversation if you want real communication. As a teacher of primary students, I learned to give them a signal – a cute sign on my desk – that let them know when I was available to listen to their anecdotes. If the sign was not up, I was only available to help with classwork. They loved it! When I was available to listen, they knew I would not be doing anything else while they talked to me. They had my undivided attention.

On the other hand, I remember once talking with my mother on the phone; I was very upset, to the point of crying. Suddenly I realized she wasn't really hearing me; you know that feeling. I said, sniffling, "Mom, what are you doing?" Her reply was, "Oh, go on talking; I was just writing my friend a letter." I was outraged! I was tearfully relating an awful incident, and she wasn't really listening – she was only hearing. Fortunately we can laugh about it now.

Real communication requires mutually giving and receiving both understanding and acceptance, if not agreement. If there is no agreement, and all that happens is that each person gains a deeper understanding of the other's viewpoint, real communication has still occurred as long as the disagreement has allowed each other to "save face."

Conversation is a pleasant, enjoyable interaction. My conversations with some friends are made of their words and my words, usually taking turns to speak. We do not always communicate, but we do connect because we each know we have been "heard." I say what I want to say about whatever I am thinking, and she says whatever she wants to say about whatever she is thinking – small talk.

Truthfully, I really dislike most "small talk." Most conversations with acquaintances, in my experience, are just that. We talk about small things – other people, places, and stuff. Talk about ideas, opinions, beliefs, current issues, art, music, sports, politics, religion. These are "big talk" – loaded topics that require genuine communication, intelligence, and information, thus are often avoided.

Likewise, some conversations are 80% their words and 20% my words. At the end of the conversation they may say, "What a great conversation we had," but all I can think is, "You are a good talker and I am a good listener." There was very little communication because there was little COMMON sharing, little MUTUAL acceptance, understanding, and meekness. He or she talked; I listened. I may indeed know more about what kind of person he is, but all he knows about me is that I am a good listener. By the way, the reverse often happens, too!

Some so-called authority on the topic suggested that older singles should look for a partner who is a good conversationalist above all other traits; you can usually talk when you can't do much else. I have a feeling that even as I advance in age, I would still like to be in a relationship with a man who can do more than talk – a man who can actually communicate would still be preferable. That means he listens to what I have to say with understanding, acceptance, and meekness.

Words are powerful, beyond our awareness of their power. The Bible says that in our words lies the power of life and death! God spoke the world into existence, it says, believe it or not. Words originate with thoughts; words can stir up emotions and feed our feelings and inspire actions. We usually speak what we really believe; we usually say what we mean and mean what we say. Rarely do we say one thing and mean another; if we do, that's called sarcasm! Even humor has an element of truth in it; otherwise it would have no impact, no meaning. Words can help us laugh at ourselves, not take ourselves so seriously, and lighten our load. Words paint pictures and help us dream dreams; words can also keep us imprisoned in the past. I want to use words powerfully AND positively in my life.

The Conditions of Unconditional Love

Remember the song "Love is a Many-Splendored Thing?" The word "love" in New Testament Greek has many forms, depending on what is loved. In the English language, we say we love God, mom, our friends, the dog, math, and pizza! We use the same word for all kinds of love.

Love has many definitions and descriptions. Love can change; love can die. Love has time limits and space boundaries. Love is an action and a feeling. Most of all, I believe love is a choice, a commitment.

How many teenagers have sworn their love for each other, but by the next weekend things have changed, and they choose someone else to love? Or a woman falls in love, gets married, returns from the honeymoon, only to awaken to reality – and the realization that the person she married is not the man she thought he was. Or a couple is married for 50 years, the husband dies, and she marries someone else. Human love is not at all like God's love.

Only God can truly love unconditionally, and only when we are being most like God can we love with very FEW conditions. But in my experience, I believe that humans are incapable of truly loving others unconditionally. If it were possible, what a wonderful world this would be!

I said to my first husband with all the love you can imagine, "There is nothing you can ever do that would make me stop loving you." I meant it with all of my being. I felt good saying that. I believed all he needed was to be loved unconditionally. I hoped it would motivate him to stop drinking and drugging. We had a baby, and I thought he would change for the baby's sake if not for mine, but he still didn't stop. We got a divorce, but he still didn't stop. Finally, years later and three wives and another son later, he stopped, thanks only to God through AA. I eventually stopped FEELING that love for him. I didn't think I could. But I did.

Love has conditions because love is a choice. It isn't based on a feeling; feelings can change. It isn't based on looks; looks can change. It really isn't based on behavior; behavior can change. It is based on a decision, and even decisions can be changed. Treat me badly enough for long enough, and I will decide to stop feeling love for you. We are built that way on purpose.

My second husband's mother told me repeatedly, but sadly, "Mick [not his real name] is really difficult to love." Wow. I thought, until that statement, that a mother's love was closest to God's unconditional love. Not true. How can anyone who has carried a life inside her body say such a thing? A mother's love is not inherently unconditional. I didn't think I could love another human being as much as I loved my son, and in my own experience, it seemed to be the closest thing to God's love, but that is not the experience of every human being.

There is a reason God is the only one who can truly love us unconditionally – without being loved first or loved back at all. He is God! He created us as we are. If anyone else could love us as God does, we would have no need of God; we would "worship" that other person.

So what did I really mean when I said to a man, "I love you"? Maybe it meant I wanted him physically. Maybe it meant I needed him emotionally. Maybe it meant I just enjoyed his company. Maybe it meant I admired him. Maybe it meant I wanted something from him – a form of unconscious manipulation. Maybe it meant I accepted him as he was. Maybe it meant nothing much at all – it was just my words said in response to his words. I don't know. Maybe it was some combination of all those meanings.

What I do know for sure is love can change. It can die or grow; it can weaken or deepen. It can be expressed differently. It can encompass many people over many years. There is room in my heart for many kinds of love, for many people. Feelings of love can overflow, and at times, seem to barely exist.

Love that lasts is a choice of my will, not just an emotional response. One country songwriter questioned whether he really loved the woman or just loved how he felt when he was with her. He asked, "Am I in love with her or in love with love?"

I try to look for reasons to keep on loving that person, not reasons to stop. I try to accept their flaws, mistakes, and goofs with the same acceptance I need from them. I NO longer accept abusive behavior of any kind. I must have boundaries to protect the one person I am supposed to love most and always – ME!

I believe our souls are made up of three parts: our minds [the heart or motivational center], our wills [decision-maker], and our emotions. We think, we decide, we feel. Our souls are the eternally real expression of who we are; our bodies are temporary.

Our minds control our bodies – some organs are controlled automatically without need for thought. Some body parts respond only to thought. Our emotions are reactions to thoughts, regardless of whether the thoughts are "true" or "real." I cry reading a book; I cry watching a movie created by technology and computer-generated animation. My tears are not able to determine truth from fiction. This makes the profession of acting possible!

We make a million decisions a day, without thinking that we are thinking! All movement is the result of electrical impulses sent from our brains to the necessary muscles. We choose to make those movements if our bodies work as they should. We decide about so many things – what to eat, what to wear, where to go, how to spend our free time throughout the waking hours of our day. We also decide what to think – we accept or reject certain ideas, images, choices. All of life is a series of choices.

Even our emotions are controlled by our minds. I know this from my own experience! My dad only spanked me three times in my entire life, each time because I mouthed off to my mother. The last time was when I was about ten years old. He held me by one arm, and as we were going around in circles, he flailed at my backside, and I cried loudly. Suddenly I decided I was not going to cry or react at all to this humiliating and degrading interaction. Enough was enough. I stiffened up, thrust my free arm straight down by my side, and calmly asserted to him, "You can beat me to death if you want to, but I am not going to cry another cry." He flailed at me a few more times, but I think my silence, punctuated by his hand smacking me at regular intervals, was too much for him. He stopped and never spanked me again.

Perhaps the love of grandchildren for their grandparents is close to unconditional love. I never saw or heard anything from any of my grandparents when I was a child that tainted my love for any of them. There were times when I heard my parents criticize one or more of them, but apparently I dismissed it as invalid. I could not list a single character defect any of them had until I was an adult, and then it was only because my parents or others told me of actions which obviously indicated some defects. I loved my grandparents so much – all four of them! That gives me hope that perhaps my grandchildren will forgive me my character defects as well. Their love is a treasure I value above all earthly things.

When I say I love someone "unconditionally" I mean I "accept" them just as they are. In fact, I believe I can "love" every human being on the face of the earth "unconditionally." They do not need to change one bit to suit me. They have my "permission" to be exactly who they are, to do whatever they choose, and I gladly assert it is none of my business unless they break the law of the land. I do not mean that I agree that their actions are good or right. Their behavior is not mine to control or criticize.

The conditions I set come in when someone wants to have more than a "stranger passing on the street" relationship with me! That's when I establish MY boundaries of what is acceptable for this relationship to grow. If, at any point I decide that I cannot fully accept something about the other person, I must move on. I don't need to try to change them, talk about it, figure it out, work it out, or wait it out. I just move on! I can "love others unconditionally" meaning "totally accept them," as long as we agree on the boundaries. Love has conditions. I set them. You set them. "Come live in my heart and pay no rent." But if you want to live in my house, we need to talk!

Fight or Flight?

I recoiled when my husband raised his voice in anger or frustration. I cringed when he swore. I found myself literally balled up in an armchair, frozen, afraid to move or breathe. I expected something worse to happen. He was going to hit me, I just knew it.

The first one did. The second husband screamed, yelled, cursed, and threatened vehemently. After he threatened to kill me in an angry fit I faced the facts and left. He had already confided in a friend at work years earlier that he wanted to kill me. The friend revealed that information to me because he was concerned my husband would carry it out and he would feel guilty for not warning me. My husband later bragged that in thirty years he had "never once hit that woman." That reminds me of Clinton's brag – "I didn't have sex with that woman." They depersonalized both of us with the phrase "that woman."

From the first husband, I learned how to run; from the second one, I learned how to stand my ground and fight back with words. The first one was an active alcoholic; he had a sickness which controlled him. The second one was not a drinker, but he had a mental disorder as well. Those are not excuses for their behavior; nothing can nullify the consequences, but I understand the reasons for it. I can forgive them with the same compassion I have for anyone who has a disease which controls them. I must constantly say to myself, "He was in more pain than any pain he inflicted on me."

With both of them, I made lists of what I would take if I had varying amounts of time to leave – a day, half a day, an hour – I could prioritize my stuff well. If I wasn't able to actually leave physically, I could "leave" emotionally by mentally making my getaway lists.

While making plans to leave, I knew I was drowning in my fantasy world when I also began making unrealistic plans for our future. In reality I really expected there to be no future at all for me so what was the harm in dreaming? It had been my route of escape for a lifetime. I had always drowned my sorrows in books and food!

The evidence of my own sickness was that my plans included the husband! We would remodel the house, take a grand vacation, start a business, or even move into a new house. I was incapable of making realistic plans for myself in the event I actually left.

What insanity I lived!

So what to do when faced with an angry, violently abusive spouse? The church I grew up in and belonged to during the first marriage had strict policies against divorce and remarriage. I felt trapped. I became suicidal as if that was the only way out. Flight seemed the only answer, but suicide ...

I left my husband, left the church, and got a divorce.

Second verse, same as the first ...

I married number two five years later only to discover that I had jumped from the "frying pan into the fire." He was even worse. His anger was first directed at my seven-year-old son. Now I was confronted with a real dilemma: to be labeled a two-time loser with two failed marriages and therefore prove to everyone that I was unworthy of a "good" man, in addition to ruining my career in Christian schools, where I had already had to give account for the failure of the first marriage in order to be hired!

In those days divorce was much less acceptable in the Christian community than it is now, but it was fairly easy to demonstrate that I was indeed the "innocent party" – a ridiculous label – since my first husband was a full-blown alcoholic.

Question: who hates divorce and the devastation it causes more – the person who has been in a successful long-term marriage or the one who has experienced the pain of it? Answer: duh. Yes, I have had bad judgment twice, admittedly. I am on a quest to find out what caused me to choose men who had bad tempers and wanted me dead!

I just wanted to love and be loved. So shoot me.

Friends, Romans, countrymen: lend me your ears!

[Antony, "Julius Caesar," act 3, scene 2, Shakespeare]

Tell everyone! Shout it from the rooftops! Al-Anon [or _____ fill in the blank!!] is the answer for whatever is wrong with your family! I wonder why this is such a secret? Why doesn't everyone know about how great Al-Anon is?

Maybe we should take out an ad in the paper, buy a billboard for a month, get business cards and flyers. Promote this thing! I didn't even know it existed thirty years ago when I really needed it. Use those catchy phrases, create a memorable character and a logo, sing a lively tune, use eye-grabbing colors and patterns. Everyone needs to know about this!

Maybe we can appeal to parents of alcoholics, children of alcoholics, spouses of alcoholics, friends and relatives of alcoholics! If that doesn't work, we can always use bribery, shock, and controversy to draw a crowd. You know, bait and switch. Advertisers are geniuses at promotion. People are hurting all over the world and they need what we have found. Right?

Ah, hold your horses, John Wayne! The Twelve Traditions are a genius plan for AA and Al-Anon, and Tradition Eleven says "attraction TO the group, not promotion OF the group." And it really is the best policy!

So don't hire a promoter, rent a sign, or buy an ad. It's a lot harder, but simpler and cheaper than that, to attract others who are hurting to begin the Al-Anon program [or to attend your church ...]

Attraction.

That means I have to live it, walk the talk, be an example, work the program for MYSELF and just share my experience, strength, and hope. Simply difficult.

That is what my Christian faith is all about, NOT as much talking the message as walking the message. It's much harder to do that. Jesus said that if HE would be lifted up – both on the cross and in our walk of faith – HE would draw ALL people to Himself. HE does the drawing because we have "glorified" Him – we have bragged about Him with our changed lives!

AA and Al-Anon are similar. I saw the changed person my first husband has become. I saw what his program has done for him. I saw it in his life, not just heard it in his words. I marveled at the genuine change. I am impressed by his courage and newly acquired wisdom. Is he perfect? Not by a long shot! But he has influenced many, he has maintained a stable marriage for over thirty years [granted his wife needs a lot of the credit], and he has won the respect of his family and the community. His actions on a daily basis speak more loudly than any words possibly could.

Walking the talk speaks volumes!

Great Expectations = Premeditated Resentments

"I thought you'd help me ..." [He lied to me.]

"I expected you to call ..." [He doesn't care.]

"I hoped you'd invite me ..." [I'm not loved.]

"I thought you'd visit me ..." [You forgot about me.]

"Don't you know what to do?" [I am incompetent.]

"That's not what I wanted ... " [You don't know me.]

"I thought you would have ..." [No common sense!?]

"I didn't think you'd ..." [You have no morals.]

Expectations are simply expecting - hoping, planning, wishing, desiring, wanting, thinking, imagining, guessing – others to do something we want them to do. Resentments develop when they don't. We are disappointed at first, but over time, we become offended; hurt feelings reign; distorted thinking sets in and the roots of bitterness grow deep.

Why do I have these expectations of others? It must have to do with having a desire to control others. Is it perhaps my own lack of worthiness, feelings of rejection, or self-righteousness?

"I WOULD have done everything expected of ME," I think. (Oh really? Let's survey your friends!)

"I always keep MY word, MY promises," I reply. (Wow! You must be a god-like creature!)

Expectations are a form of manipulation and management. I have decided what you should do or be or say, and I will do everything in my power to make you do or be or say what I want you to do or be or say.

God is a much nicer Being than that!

He gives us free will without manipulating or managing. Contrary to popular opinion, GOD does not have any expectations of us. He is God; He knows everything. I cannot disappoint Him. He is not shocked, surprised, or hurt by my actions. He gives me choices which He clearly tells me have consequences, good or bad, and He allows me to choose – freely.

Not surprisingly, He already knows what I will choose. He accepts me just as I am. If only I could really be more like God – really like His character – instead of trying to be a god-like creature - who is totally unlike my real Higher Power.

On the other hand, I have a right to set certain parameters for our relationship. I have a right to decide the objective conditions for our relationship; I do not need to be your doormat in order to have a relationship with you. And I can set boundaries – "my rules of engagement." These are not expectations; they are deal breakers!

Heaven or Hell?

Is there a heaven on earth or a hell to pay? The answer is yes to both, and I can choose either.

But for now it's all in my own head! Just wandering through my head is about the most dangerously scary thing I have ever done. An AA friend says, "Don't go into that neighborhood without an escort! It's a dangerous place." Another friend put it this way, "Don't go there without a bodyguard and a flashlight." There are many versions of this warning.

I am learning the wisdom of those suggestions. Recently I was fortunate enough to spend six months over the winter in Florida with my brother. He lives on a beautiful lake designated a bird sanctuary. The weather, the water, and the winged creatures I love so much created a post card scene every day for me as I sat overlooking the lake from my brother's screened patio. I loved sitting out there to do my daily reading and journal writing, listening to oldies on the radio, even sipping a cup of coffee while wrapped in a blanket on a chilly morning. It was idyllic.

One morning I was blinded to the beauty. I was on a hike through my head without the necessary protective equipment, and I was under mental assault. My anguish was real, my pain was real, my emotions were all over the place. Suddenly it occurred to me. I opened my eyes, both the physical ones and the spiritual ones, and I saw the peaceful beauty that had been there every day. It varied at times – the water rippled or lay still as glass, the sky was blue tinged with clouds or crystal clear, occasionally a little rain punctured the surface of the water. The same two furry gray squirrels scurried after each other, up one live oak tree and down the other. The same three otters swam by, making their daily rounds of the lake. Blue herons, jet black crows, white swans, and northern geese swooped over the water.

It was a heavenly scene, but I was hiking through hell ... inside my own head. I was in a war zone, on the front lines, but the war had ended. The truce had been signed, and nobody told me. I looked around. I was alone, physically, but what a bloody battle was going on in my hellish head! That group called "they" were there in full force, armed with all their usual ammo and weapons. My three-ugly step-sisters – Shoulda, Woulda, and Coulda - were yakking their heads off while the bullets and bombs flew from every direction. I was assaulted by all the debris of the past, the imagined land mines of the future, and I felt helplessly trapped.

It was then that I realized it was all in my head, not the abuse or the bad decisions or the financial problems or the questions about tomorrow. Those were real. It was the suffering, the anguish, the worry, the fear, the guilt, the bitterness, the resentment, the desire for revenge, the humiliation of it all that was alive in my head. I had the power to defeat them all. I could choose to reject those thoughts, those bad memories, those fears – all of it!

Here I was – surrounded by beauty, with all my needs met, physically safe, healthy, comfortable, and nothing to worry about. I had no job but my obligations were being met, I had no home of my own but I had a roof over my head and a bed to sleep in. I was with someone who cared about me and would not allow me to be hurt again.

The war was only going on in my head. It was over. It was the Past. Done. No new war had been declared. And I could choose to be neutral. I am now determined to be a human neutral zone, giving no aid, no money, no arms, no ammo, no training. I can choose peace at all costs. I can be happy every day. I can live in heaven on earth. Hell has already been paid.

Too many people are waiting until after death to enjoy their "resurrection lives." The promises of heaven are no more tears, no more pain, no more death, no more sorrow, no more darkness. I now know I can begin my resurrection life now – I can change my thinking so that I have fewer tears, less pain, no fear of death, less sorrow, and I can live in the light of His Truth.

Why wait for heaven? It can begin now.

How I Happily Flunked People - Pleasing 101

I was proud of being a "people-pleaser" until I realized I had not been successful at it. In fact, my AA friend suggested that I write down all the people whom I had attempted to please over my lifetime, and ask each of them if I had been successful. I figured a passing grade would mean 70% of them would agree that indeed I had pleased them. As I seriously considered actually asking some of them how well I had done, I remembered an experience I had had teaching in a private school in Texas and changed my mind.

I was teaching fifth grade, a class of about 25 students from upper middle class families in the Dallas area. I really enjoyed these kids! It was my second year in the school, and with over ten years of experience under my belt, I had confidence that I was a competent teacher. I had always gotten good evaluations and had corrected any areas that needed attention. It was conference time, and I was looking forward to meeting one father. He was an architect, a career path I toyed with briefly. His son in my class was a bright young man, sporting a shock of blond hair and icy blue eyes, I suspected he had inherited from an equally handsome father. Ryan [not his real name] was smart, but he wanted perfect grades on spelling tests. I had discovered his ingenious cheating scheme, and gave him the standard consequences – demerits. I liked Ryan, and in my mind, the incident was over.

I was shocked, therefore, when the father began our meeting with the following statement: "You are not fit to teach anywhere, let alone in a [private] school." The meeting got worse. I suggested several alternatives: that he see the principal, move his son to another classroom, sit in my class to observe, and as a last resort, suggested he might want to find another school. He refused to do any of those things. Finally, his wife took pity on me and suggested that perhaps [duh] he was being a bit too harsh. The meeting ended. They did not take my suggestions, and Ryan stayed in my class without further incident.

The real dilemma was the next parent. Her daughter Sharon [not her real name] could not have loved me more, and the mother insisted that I was a God-sent angel, the best thing that could have happened to her daughter. She gushed with praise for everything!

Same teacher – me – in the same classroom! Two students, both very bright, from good families, with entirely different perspectives. How could that be?

The lesson I learned that day was this. I was neither a devil nor an angel. I was merely a human being doing the best I could to teach these children. What these parents did not know, and the first one did not bother to consider, was that ALL teachers are just flawed human beings doing the best they can on any given day. He had no idea what was going on in my personal life, and I doubt he would have cared. It would not have been an excuse if I had behaved unprofessionally, but the idea should have given him some compassion. After all, I had not hurt his child. He had hurt me.

How can you be the exact same person, saying all the same things, doing all the same things, and fail so miserably at pleasing one person and succeed so incredibly at pleasing another? The answer, of course, is it was their perspective, nothing to do with me.

Another biblical principle we all know is the Golden Rule: "do unto others as you want them to do unto you." You need to add "but don't expect them to!" Bend over backwards to be accommodating, help out by going the extra mile, and all you will usually get is a sore back and aching feet! Clearly we should do what's right just because it is right to do, but with all your people-pleasing efforts, remember not to neglect your own welfare in the pleasing. If you don't take care of yourself, who will? Adults look out for their own best interests; martyrs die.

My conclusion is that I have always failed at "people-pleasing" because there was one person I neglected terribly – me. Not that I have never done what I wanted to do; I have most of the time, but with anxiety, guilt, and fear that "they" were displeased!

Sure, some people think I am an angel – not really true; some think I am a devil – not true either. All that matters is this: what does God think and what do I think? Everyone else can line up on either side. With God I get an A+ because He loves me unconditionally. I give myself an O for Outstanding effort and progress!

Recently one good friend said to me, "I didn't like something you did." I was then quite interested to hear what she had to say. My opinion about my behavior is quite different from hers; in fact, I am rather pleased with myself for having the courage and honesty to do what I did, but I got another F in People-Pleasing 101. That's the way it goes. I made a decision and expressed an opinion. I made a choice. She made a choice, too. She didn't like my choice. No big deal. We all have options. We accept each other's decisions.

I am learning that I have to make decisions and choices that are best and right for me. I am allowed to choose simply based on a preference; my choices do not have to be popular. I do not have to explain my decisions or justify my actions. LIFE should not be lived as if we were on trial in a courtroom!

My question is why do I need anyone else's approval? I have God's unconditional love. It disturbs me that I crave acceptance and approval; I want to break this addiction for good. I am easily "hurt" by certain family member's "words" of personal criticism; in contrast, I can usually accept criticism related to job performance. It must be that I give the opinions of some people greater weight than others. It's a mystery I look forward to unraveling on my journey of serenity.

How to Love Your Kids . . . to Death!

Do everything for him that you possibly can to make his life easier than you had it. Manage his life, mother him well, and be sure to be a martyr who reminds him constantly of all you have sacrificed for him. This will serve you well when you need to use guilt to manipulate him.

Be sure that you spare no expense buying him lots of stuff, especially to help him keep up with his peers. You don't want him to appear to be neglected. Keep him from pain and suffering every chance you can no matter how the pain and suffering came to him, even if it was the unfortunate consequence of his own actions. You love him so much you just can't stand to see him suffer for any reason!

Compare her to anyone else who has it worse. This will be such a comfort when anything bad happens. "Cheer up! You could be as bad off as Susie down the street. Be glad you aren't her!" This will help her become arrogant and ungrateful. On the other hand, don't forget to compare her to kids her age who have life easier, as well. Remind her that they are just stuck-up snobs who don't deserve the easy life. You do deserve it, of course.

Teach him to practice lying. It will make the tough times in life so much more bearable. The lies are just little white lies, anyways. You see, a kid who can look himself in the mirror and justify his bad behavior will have less difficulty getting out of trouble with the authorities, even with God.

Encourage her to play the Blame Game. You still play it yourself at times, right? You can't help how you turned out. You didn't ask to be born. Kids are a combination of inherited traits and their environment – you have a lot to blame there. Your parents are primary culprits. After all, they created that "environment" you grew up in; you didn't. And remember, teachers and preachers have a grave responsibility for what they have taught kids or what they preached in God's name. They will be held to a higher standard. You aren't to blame – for anything!

You can't help the language he uses or the prejudices he holds. They pick up that stuff at school and from the neighbor kids. "By the way, I don't know what this neighborhood is turning into with all these d*** immigrants moving in. They sure aren't like my Scots-Irish-Native American ancestors!"

Be sure he wears the right clothes, gets into the right cliques, is on the best teams, and goes to the biggest number-one party college – all which YOU pick for him. He cannot be trusted to choose his own friends and develop his own interests. What would "they" think?

Insist that she attend the church of YOUR choice following all YOUR standards, beliefs, doctrines, and practices even after she reaches adulthood. After all, your church is the "most right and the most righteous" and all the others are hypocrites. You are an excellent hypocrite spotter, everyone knows.

Keep rescuing him - whether from financial problems, relationship problems, job problems, legal problems, and of course, from moral problems. If you have done all of the above, he will always need you . . . to rescue him.

Finally, keep telling her how she deserves better. She is entitled to so much more. The government, Grandpa, and God owe her a debt for . . . something. Life isn't fair, you know. Good luck. You will need a lot of money to keep bailing her out ... of life! And then there's the funeral cost . . .

I want to BE a PRO!

Everyone admires a pro – a professional in any arena. I can never be a pro at any sport; I consider it an accomplishment not to fall on my face walking across a room. But I have discovered I can be a pro in life – I can learn to respond to any situation in a proactive manner; I no longer have to wait for something to happen and then react. Of course, I cannot be prepared for every contingency, but "I CAN have a PLAN."

I can learn how to respond to the character defects in others, which are so easy to see, by keeping my focus on me, on my character defects so well-hidden from my own view.

The following is a comparative.look at being reactive or being proactive:

BEING REACTIVE:	BEING PROACTIVE:
It happens after the fact.	It's a planned response before the incident.

Words and actions are impulsive.	There are planned, observable outcomes.
Too often it is emotionally driven.	These responses are intellectually driven.
Reacting is driven by our senses.	These responses are logical and reasoned.
Reacting involves little thought.	Proactive responses are well thought out.
It happens quickly.	Being proactive takes time.
Reactions are forced.	Practiced responses.
Reacting is a fast-food mentality.	This is a fine-dining-with-reservations mentality.
It is stressful now, under pressure.	It is anticipated, no stress.
It is stressful, before and after.	It is decisive with no stress.
It is driven by childish motives.	By mature motives.
Reacting must be immediate.	By mature motives.
Reacting is subjective, illogical.	Logical and objective.
Reacting is not fun.	Enjoyably satisfying.

All the Al-Anon and AA slogans are ways to be proactive. They are planned responses to what others say or do, and planned responses to what my own distorted thinking tries to do to keep me miserable.

One of the best everyday ways to be proactive is at those times when someone is judgmental or offers unwanted advice. A planned, proactive response can be "I'm sorry you feel that way," or "That's an interesting idea; I will give it some thought," or "That's your opinion and you are entitled to it." We no longer have to wait for those inevitable words or actions that trigger our distorted, sick behavior and make us unhappy. We can keep our own dignity, keep our own opinions, and keep our serenity!

In Al-Anon I am learning slogans and phrases which help me be proactive when confronted with others' words and actions which used to upset me; I am not giving away my hard-earned serenity any more.

I will be a PRO!

Intimacy Doesn't Mean Sex

I was sitting with an old family friend on a bench at LAX airport waiting for my flight home. We weren't talking. There was so much to be said, and yet nothing more, really. All the important things had been said: thank-you, take-care-of-yourself, keep-in-touch, call-me-if-you-need-anything. There was nothing to do but wait. I watched as couples of all ages kissed good-by.

We just sat there, together, saying nothing. That was over twenty years ago. He was one of the most important people in my life, and I didn't know if I would ever see him again, but we said nothing. We knew what was in each other's hearts; we had a powerful connection. Years filled with hours of talk had already transpired. We were intimately connected in spirit and soul.

Intimacy is the element of relationship I desire and appreciate most. That's because my love languages are time, talk, and touch. These three, in my opinion, access body, soul, and spirit – the complete person.

Too often relationships between men and women begin at the physical level, and even more often, stay there. Even at best, getting acquainted at the spiritual, emotional, and intellectual levels requires an investment of time with no guarantee of good results.

One expert I heard speak said that we are connected on an emotional level to every person with whom we have had sexual intimacy, whether it was "recreational" or genuine "love-making." This connection affects us throughout our lives. And the Bill Clinton definition of sex does not hold up here! Let the record show, any kind of sexual intimacy IS sex. This is why molestation, rape and incest are devastating.

Even when one consents to sex with a partner, there may be elements of manipulation which may render it not really as willing for one partner as it appears to be. Women have used their feminine wiles for centuries to get something else they wanted; men have seduced women for results other than sexual pleasure.

My first marriage, admittedly when I was young and foolish, was based almost entirely on physical attraction. I thought there was more, but we never really connected spiritually, intellectually, or emotionally. We just were not "soul mates;" we were "body mates." I thought we loved each other and perhaps we did, but we did not really have emotional or spiritual intimacy. We just didn't believe the same things about life.

When a relationship is merely physical, we miss out on intimacy later because we failed to develop it in the initial stages of our relationship. It requires connection, communication, and commonality. I have often heard it said that "love is a choice, not a feeling" and I agree. Too often we get caught up in the "feeling" of being IN love; we actually fall in love with "being in love." Later, when that feeling wears thin, the honeymoon is over, and life begins, we wonder, could we have made a mistake? We wanted intimacy, but we only got sex, a roommate, and a business deal. NOT what I bargained for!

If a relationship can begin on a spiritual level [shared beliefs], then progress to the soul [shared intellectual ideas, shared drive, work ethic and emotional connections] and then finally to the body, we might have a better chance at real intimacy. So says noted speaker Bill Gothard in the Basic Youth Conflicts Seminars I attended in the late 70's. It makes sense to me now, but I have rarely had the opportunity to see it lived out in anyone's life.

One relationship I had in the 70's developed long distance, by telephone and mail, but we had never met. We talked for hours, prayed together, exchanged pictures, apparently liked each other's looks and voices [his DJ's voice would melt butter], but when we met, he looked nothing like his touched-up professional photo. I thought I knew this man; after all, we had talked for hours and written each other for months, but his true character was revealed over the course of a week when he visited in my town. I was devastated, spent as little time as possible with him, and cried on my friend's shoulder when he finally left. He had terrible manners, disgusting habits, and lacked most social skills. Physical characteristics do matter. Habits and mannerisms do matter.

I am in a long distance relationship with a man I had seen before only briefly. We have talked for thousands of hours. We have spent only a few hours together. I think we understand each other on a deeply spiritual and soulful level. We have an intimate relationship from 1,500 miles apart that I did not have living in the same house with a husband of thirty years. We've talked, laughed, cried, shared secrets. We are intimately connected . . . from a distance.

Intimacy can occur between family members, same sexes, married, unmarried, different races, nationalities, religions, creeds, economic levels, ages ... you name it! We are afraid of intimacy because it requires revealing our true selves, but genuine intimacy is so worth the effort. Nowadays sex has been reduced to nothing but a base physical act. Real connection on the levels of spirit and soul are practically non-existent.

Maybe genuine intimacy requires unselfish love and that requires real communication. Without loving respect, sex is only sex - kind of like the difference between seeing a postcard of the Grand Canyon and actually being there taking the picture! They look so much alike, but being there, experiencing it sensually, emotionally, and spiritually, cannot be duplicated on a piece of paper.

Sex is only a postcard imitation ... without genuine loving intimacy.

It's My Story and I'm Stickin' to It

I don't have to defend myself.

    Am I on trial here?

I don't have to explain myself.

    Whose approval, except my own and God's, do I need?

I don't have to answer questions except under oath.

    Have I committed a crime?

I don't have to answer phone calls.

    It's my phone, my house, my choice.

I don't have to answer the doorbell.

    It's my door, ditto.

I don't have to reply to emails.

    It's my computer and my address, ditto.

I don't have to tell everyone my truths nor do I need to tell lies. I can mind my own business and encourage others to mind theirs.

It's my story. It's my life. Who knows it better than I? Who owns the rights to it?

"It's my story and I can tell it any way I want to," my brother says. Some people are gifted with hyperbole, exaggeration, or imagination. Some are cursed with a silent tongue and cannot give voice to their pain. Some curse others with a loose one. A few people are gifted with the simplicity of a tight vocabulary; my dad was a man of few words, but his words were powerful. I'm not sure he knew that.

Lying used to bother me – other people's lies far more than my own. I, on the other hand, was a skilled liar and didn't realize it for years. I lied to myself most often, not so much to others. I hated lies; they hurt me, I thought. Other people's lies did not have the power to hurt me, however, unless I gave them that power. My own lies to myself did the most damage.

I can lie if I want to; you can lie if you want to. We will both suffer the consequences for lying, separately. If I choose to believe you and you lie to me, I will still suffer the consequences because I made a decision, a choice, to believe you. That is a very hard truth but one I have learned reluctantly over a lifetime of hurts. I still have a right to choose whom I will believe and what I will believe. Whether you lie to me or not is not my problem; whether I believe it IS my problem!

It's your story to tell, and it's mine to believe . . . or not.

Let Go and Let God.
But Who IS God?

I willingly let go of my perceived control of people, situations, the past, the future, and other things and give it to God, but who IS that? I am not going to let some entity I don't even know, can't see, can't touch, or hear be in control of MY life! No way! This seems to be the essence of my basic life dilemma – I seem eager to trust and give control to people, even myself, but I am reluctant to trust and give control to God.

Who or what is this "God of my understanding" as the Twelve Steps say?

Only I can answer that question for myself, and only you can answer that question for yourself. The trouble is that religious institutions and religious leaders attempt to answer that question for us. I allowed that to happen for most of my life, but no more. I am taking control of what I am supposed to manage – my own life ... and that includes my faith, my own belief system.

The Serenity Prayer tells me to accept what I cannot change and change what I can. The genius of that and, at the same time, the dilemma of that is figuring out which one is which – therefore wisdom is essential. I will accept without conditions everyone and everything else, including the past and its mistakes, but I will insist adamantly to be in charge of ME, MYSELF, and I – my life, my body, my beliefs, my needs, my ideas, my opinions, even my feelings!

Therefore, having said that, how do I let go and let God ... an unknown entity ... control anything? Since thousands of individuals throughout the past six decades have found peace and a happy life by surrendering their lives to this God through the Twelve Steps, perhaps I should give it some consideration. Eh?

How can God be defined so that I can recognize him, her or it? In an attempt to do just that, the Holy Bible was written by more than forty authors over a four-hundred-year period, including sixty-six books of history, prophecy, poetry, and instruction.

Millions of other books have been written over the centuries attempting to describe God. Other great religions of the world have tried to accomplish a similar task. Yet I believe the questions still cry out from the hearts of every human being in the world: Who is God? What is God? Where is God? Most importantly, what does this God have to do with me?

So, in my humble [yet ironically arrogant] opinion, here goes.

I believe God can be defined as that entity which ...

    a) you trust for your security and comfort

    b) controls you either directly or indirectly

Therefore, my god used to be my mother. I trusted her implicitly and she controlled my life completely. I am now sixty-plus years old, and I am still trying to wrench my life's control from her beautiful gnarled past-eighty-year-old hands. As they say in the South, "bless her heart."

Ideally, if parents would begin when children are very young, teaching their children HOW to think for themselves, HOW to make decisions about small things, under their loving guidance and wise protection, gradually letting go as the children grow up, there might be little need for AA or Al-Anon. Of course, that's just my opinion and my experience talking.

Parents act like god-like creatures in their children's lives and some never figure out how then to surrender control to these individuals, and OMG, surrender control to GOD? Are you kidding? I AM GOD in their lives! I created their bodies – (OK, my sexual partner and I did) – I fed them, clothed them, gave them shelter, educated them, protected them!! Let go and let ... WHO? I hope you get the point.

The basic ideas I learned about God as a child were a) that He was watching me [the Big Eye in the Sky] and b) that He would punish me for doing anything wrong [as defined by my mother and her church]. He had rules I had better follow, but if I would be a "good girl" [as defined by my mother and her church] God would reward me with a good life. Fear is a weak motivator, but it works if you live in the same house with "god!"

Children naturally want to please their parents, I think, and they learn very early in life what it takes, or they learn it will be impossible, so they rebel or leave. "Fight or flight" is human nature's way of survival. Sometimes "flight" is expressed as passivity, retreat, surrender, giving in, giving up. I used to equate that kind of passivity with the idea of "acceptance" I later learned in Al-Anon. I was so wrong - not true at all!

There was little chance for me to rebel or fight, so retreat – flight – was my only option. I retreated into myself, into my imagination, into books. Couple that with living under a religious order that prohibited me from playing a musical instrument, participating in sports because I could wear only dresses and skirts, joining clubs like Girl Scouts, dancing, going to movies, and you have an overweight, over-protected, well-behaved reclusive bookworm with incredibly good grades. I could therefore please my mother!

I could never please my dad because of those very same things I did to escape – I was a dreamer, he said, which meant I spent my time in what he saw as useless endeavors, and I was getting fat, which must have been equal in his mind to going to hell in a hand basket! He wanted me to be skinny, and I wasn't. At sixteen, I weighed 155 lbs and wore a size 13 dress when I got my driver's license. Crime of the century!

I have spent most of my life trying to keep my mother's approval and earn my dad's. My dad died when I was 49 and I still wasn't skinny; my mom – the jury is still out on that one. (HA!) They were basically good loving parents, but still lacked some parenting skills, still employed some distorted thinking patterns, and therefore produced flawed children. By the way, ALL of us humans are flawed and we have ALL in turn produced flawed off-spring.

Now what shall I, and my off-spring, do about our flaws? That is my life's journey – seeking sanity with serenity. What does all that have to do with letting go and letting God? Everything, in my opinion.

I developed a distorted image of God, therefore a distorted way of looking at life, and in turn irrational methods for solving life's problems. Human nature still dictates flight or fight, but I fought when I should have walked away. I ran away when I should have stayed and fought for my "self."

I also developed a distorted view of God and what my relationship to Him is. Was He really the big eye in the sky Who would punish me for being what He created me to be – a human being?

NOW my view of God, whom I trust explicitly and implicitly, is that He ...

> 1) loves me unconditionally 100% of the time because He created me,
>
> 2) has my best interests at heart in all areas of my life,
>
> 3) knows all about me, past, present, and future,
>
> 4) cannot be surprised, disappointed, impressed, confused, or stumped by my behavior or thoughts,
>
> 5) watches over me and, as a perfect parent, only permits things to happen to me for my ultimate good,
>
> 6) is completely in charge of the universe, yet gives each of us the free will to make our own choices,
>
> 7) teaches us what we ultimately need to know and do to have the best life possible.

Every day my prayer is what Step 11 says: I pray only to know God's will for my life and to have the power to carry it out today. At the end of the day, my prayer is one of gratitude for whatever happened because I trusted Him to carry out His own will, either for my blessing or a lesson.

I am learning to let go of my feeble efforts to control things which are none of my business and working to change what is my business - me.

Life is so much easier; I am more peaceful; I am happier every day. The God of my understanding is doing a wonderful job with my life! I think I'll keep on letting go and letting God!

Live and let Live . . . and Be Nice About It!

Live – that's my job.

Let live – that's your job and everyone else's job.

Be nice about it – that's my job.

Does this mean that I have to move into the wilderness, become an anti-social hermit, and never interact with other humans? I've given it serious consideration, and it might be a good idea for anyone who can't seem to "live and let live."

What exactly does it mean to live and let live? It's another way of looking at "mind your own business." If you love the drama of being in the middle of other people's lives, perhaps this idea is for you. Getting into triangular relationships, sometimes called "getting in the middle," is just trying to help, you may think. One rule of thumb for knowing when to get into the problem is the old adage: "If I am not part of the problem or part of the solution, it is none of my business." For some people who love the drama, this too can be unclear. I think I AM part of the solution – if only they would just do what I tell them to do! Or ... my friend dragged me into it, and now I AM part of the problem, too. Exactly how did your friend "drag" you into it? Needless to say, it was juicy gossip that did the dragging.

Gossip is so ugly. It has many faces. Sometimes the motives behind gossip are jealousy or low self-esteem. Sometimes getting involved in other people's drama is a substitute for dealing with your own issues, an attempt to deflect attention away from yourself. Sometimes well-meaning people are just busybodies wearing the mask of Christian prayer and concern. Prayer request time in a children's Sunday School class or in a women's Bible class can be very revealing -- a form of gossip, and those who listen often never really pray for those mentioned. Some people are just plain nosy, collectors of trivial information about other people, because other people's lives are more interesting than their own. Some are just control freaks who get into other people's problems because they are so powerless in their own.

LIVE . . . live your own life to the fullest. Enjoy finding out who YOU are. It's a fascinating discovery! You will LIKE what you discover, I promise. God created you to be you, the only one in the universe, ever. As one AA friend said to me, "Be yourself because everyone else is taken!" You are unique; no one else is exactly like you, and no one else can discover who you really are, completely. Explore your own interests, abilities, opinions, beliefs, and yes, defects of character which God will correct with your cooperation one at a time.

I have been on this journey for a while, and I have begun several journals of what I now believe about God, religion, politics, and life. I am exploring so many facets of my personality; I have discarded many things I once believed about myself, about God, about politics, about life in general that it feels like I am starting over – that NEW life, that new beginning I always wanted, and I am the only one in charge of it. No one else can LIVE my life.

LET LIVE . . . get so involved with this adventure of discovery – discovering who you are – that you won't even want to be in on other people's drama. Your own life will be so interesting that other people's drama will seem dull in comparison. Minding my own business is a full-time adventure, not just a dreary job, and I think I am the most fascinating person I know. That is not arrogance; it is humility at its genuine best. God gave me one person to be my best friend for life and neglecting her by dabbling in everyone else's life is a crime. She and I will be together 24/7 for life, and throughout eternity, I believe. I will nurture her, love her, be gentle and kind with her. She is my only real BFF for life. She is ME!

You there, go live your life, and if our lives cross paths, I will rejoice, but if they do not, I will still rejoice for us both. My own life is that good . . . today!

Living IN Today, Anticipating Tomorrow

I must really be nuts because I have always had trouble living IN today; I worried about tomorrow and fretted over mistakes of the past. I was seldom really "IN the moment." Think about the contradiction of NOT living IN today. What other time period can I live in? Is time travel possible? No! How absurd to talk about not living in today. The realization of my absurdity was the first step in learning to let go - of yesterday AND tomorrow. Holding onto yesterday is like gathering ashes in a windstorm; fretting about tomorrow is akin to trying to grasp the wind itself.

I began to meditate on a sentence from Psalm 118:24, "This is the day the Lord has made; I will rejoice and be glad in it." After reading it daily for several weeks, it suddenly occurred to me that it was true EVERY DAY. It never said "Yesterday WAS the day the Lord made ..." or

"Tomorrow WILL BE the day the Lord makes ..." It said the same thing every day. THIS day – today – IS the day for me to rejoice and be glad - IN THIS day.

I used to put off my life until my circumstances changed. They were better sometimes and then they'd get worse. I always found some excuse for not fully, completely, unreservedly enjoying every day. I actually felt guilty for being happy if my circumstances were not perfect, like feeling guilty for laughing at a funeral! I wanted to be happy, but what would "They" think?

"How can she be happy now? She doesn't even have a job! How can she be happy when she doesn't even have a home! No job, no money, no home, living with family, twice divorced, alienated from her church, of no use to society at all! Is she INSANE? Being happy? Smiling? Even belly laughing -- in 'pub-lic'...?"

I finally asked myself four questions:

WHEN would I be permitted to enjoy my life everyday?

WHO would grant me that great privilege?

WHAT circumstances would finally allow it?

WHY would it be permissible then?

God, through Al-Anon, answered all my questions:

When? Now and every day!

Who says it's OK? Me! I choose!

What circumstances? In ALL circumstances.

Why? It is the will of God!

Now let's talk about each of these answers.

It is the will of God that each of us is genuinely happy, content, and serene every day IN the middle of all our circumstances – IN the middle of all the trouble which surrounds us, overwhelms us, and tries to defeat us because He has promised, "I – God – will never leave you nor forsake you," no matter what happens.

I am the only one who can decide to be happy or not. "Happiness is an inside job," an AA and Al-Anon slogan says. There are people I know personally and those I see in the news whose "circumstances" seem perfect, but who are miserably suicidal, deliberately or slowly.

I am so weary of the attitude, "Life is hard, but at least we will go to heaven when we die. Sigh." That is like sitting down to a feast and choosing only the crumbs! Life IS a feast, and I have too long settled for leftovers. I have less time ahead of me than there is behind me, but I can choose to be deliriously happy on the last day of my life.

God promises joy today in the middle of whatever hells I create for myself! I – just me – I decide about my joy. Psalm 139 says, "If I make my bed in hell, God is there." God is with me to empower me with peace during the storm, not only after the storm passes.

How can I have joy in the middle of tremendous loss? Round up everyone you know who has ever endured and survived a crisis. Ask them how it happened, and I'll bet they will say, "I had to get a new perspective, get my priorities right, count my blessings." THEY had to do it;

THEY had to change; THEY had to choose. God is the power source; we just need to get plugged in!

I know, I KNOW, maintaining a state of euphoria 24/7 would actually be the manic state of bipolar disorder. Of course, no one can rationally or healthfully maintain such a state, but one can CHOOSE joy, peace, contentment, or satisfaction under any circumstance.

"I choose joy," writes Max Lucado in the journal Grace for the Moment. He writes, "I choose joy. I will invite my God to be the God of circumstance. I will refuse the temptation to be cynical ... the tool of the lazy thinker. I will refuse to see people as anything less than human beings created by God. I will refuse to see any problem as anything less than an opportunity to see God!"

Choosing and refusing are words of our will, our decision-making center, and within our own power to exercise. I am encouraged and empowered to know that I can refuse or choose to have a good day! I CAN, and I need no permission from "Them".

We live in a culture which promotes competition, defines a man's worth and happiness by his bank account and possessions. We strangely pity but secretly envy the person who is happy in spite of their lack. How dare they be so happy in the midst of their loss? What a heartless creature to smile when things are going awry! I have heard people comment about the innocent joy and pure faith of a retarded woman as if these qualities are related somehow to her mental deficiencies. Is that insanity or serenity? Oh, that I could be just like her!

Me No Speaky Your Language

Dr. Gary Chapman wrote a fascinating and practical book on what he calls the five love languages. He maintains that there are five major ways in which we RECEIVE love or EXPRESS love, whether with children, parents, friends, or spouse:

1. TIME - Spending quality time together
2. TALK - Speaking positive words
3. TOUCH - Touching comfortably
4. SERVICE - Doing acts of service
5. GIFTS - Giving gifts of money or things

Most of us can identify our love language simply by noticing what action makes us FEEL loved.

If he just tells you what a wonderful person you are, and you tend to do similar things with those you love, your love language is positive words. If he seems to enjoy going places with you, doing the same things you do, your love language is quality time. If he is a touchy-feely person –

well, it's obvious his love language is touch. If he likes to wait on you hand and foot, run errands for you, make your favorite breakfast and bring it to you in bed, then his love language is doing acts of service. Finally, if he showers you with gifts of candy and flowers and perfume, you have a guy with the love language of giving gifts.

Most of us have more than one, but one language is dominant. Remember, this is about FEELING loved and EXPRESSING love – a two-way street. Problems occur when each person in a marriage has a different love language. Naturally, you told each other at least once that you loved each other and you got married. But now he never tells you you're pretty or wants to talk. He used to be such a good listener, and he always seemed to like how you looked. Time and positive talk must be your love language but they are not really his.

My last husband's love language was doing deeds of service and perhaps giving gifts. Every time we had an argument he "apologized" by sending me flowers at work or doing all the little chores around the house he knew I wanted done. Only my co-workers were impressed by the flowers, and I could have hired someone to do the repairs. I wanted an "intimate relationship." I wanted to spend time talking and taking walks, holding hands; even a love note would have impressed me. He did choose beautiful cards, but they were not HIS words. We didn't speak each other's love languages. Bad combination. I suppose he did love me in his dysfunctional way, but "me no speaky his language."

These problems are not impossible to overcome by gaining awareness, giving acceptance, and taking action. Discover your love languages, accept the differences, and learn how to speak your partner's language. You would do as much if you fell in love with someone who spoke French, wouldn't you? Of course, it would take time and practice and patience and humor to actually learn to speak French fluently, but eventually you would because of your great love. And life would be more satisfying and a bit easier; your love for each other might be deepened with appreciation for the effort you exerted. And it can only deepen your ability to communicate.

The same is true for the effort, time, patience, practice, and humor needed to learn your partner's love language. It doesn't happen overnight. You will make mistakes. You will get better at it with practice and time. And a good sense of humor will make it worth your effort. To know that your partner, not only knows intellectually that you love him, but FEELS it in a way he never did before, has got to be reward enough. Much of what we do in relationships with parents, children, even friends is aimed at insuring that they FEEL our love for them. Hallmark and American Greetings are built on the need we have to EXPRESS love in a way that makes others FEEL loved.

Your alcoholic may not express love in your language, but you will be pleasantly surprised by how much it improves your relationship to express love to him in his.

Meet My Ugly Step-Sisters of the If-Only Family

What a family! Poor Cinderella had it tough. Her story was my favorite fairy tale for my entire childhood. She was mistreated by her step-mother, which forever gave step-parents a bad name, and to add insult to injury, she was mistreated by her ugly step-sisters. All I want to know is, "Where the heck was Dad?" My ugly step-sisters, Shoulda, Woulda, and Coulda, are no better.

Fast forward to Mr. Job in the Bible. What a guy! Here is a real person whose story is the oldest book of the Bible. Job is revered for his patience, but the real mystery to me is what he did that apparently ended his misery and restored him to prosperity and good health. When he prayed for his friends, God restored to him twice what he had lost! What miserable friends he had! No wonder he is known as the "Father of Patience." His patience, I think, was not in enduring his pain and loss, but in putting up with his friends! And don't forget that cranky wife of his!

Just like Miss Cinderella, Job had some people goading him. Cinderella had to listen to her step-sisters' diatribes about their unfounded hopes of winning the prince; Job had to listen to his miserable friends try to figure out what caused his misery and how he could get out of it. Since when can miserable people give advice about how to get out of misery?

Both Job and Cinderella were trapped and suffering, and the last thing they needed to hear was, "You should have done this ... you could have done that ... if only you would have done what I said ..." and my personal favorite, "Let me tell you what you ought to do." Job's wife was a real gem because her advice to Job was, "Curse God and die!" What love and devotion! That would certainly have ended his misery – forever.

I am amazed that people think they are actually being helpful to say such things. My sweet dad was closely related, I think, to the "If-Only" family. He rarely had anything to say before I made a decision, but he brought all the "sisters" to the table after I messed up; and my brother "Oughta" used to start every sentence with "Let me tell ya what ya oughta do."

Who would have thought that Cinderella and Job had common relatives, huh? Both had great endings to their stories, and all for one reason. Neither of them allowed their friends' and families' negativity to affect them. They accepted it for what it was, and Job even prayed for his well-meaning friends. Neither of them attempted revenge, argued the injustice of their situations, threatened, whined, cried, fretted, or called the local TV news station to do a pity story on them. Wow!

Whether you believe Cinderella was real or Job was not, the moral of the story is the same. Acceptance is the key to serenity. And the ultimate example is Jesus who, as he hung dying on the cross, prayed, "Father, forgive them because they don't know what they are doing" – forgiving them for what some might consider the worst crime in the history of the world! Forgiveness, acceptance, understanding, self-assured confidence in what He had chosen to do, in spite of public opinion.

I may not always agree with our Presidents, but they must exhibit confidence in their own decision-making ability, before and after the fact, in order to keep their own sanity and to keep their jobs! Can you imagine a President who whined and vacillated publicly over every decision? What a joke!

Understanding and non-judgmental acceptance of other people's well-intentioned or evil-intentioned opinionated advice is good for me in the long run. It can also be good for my self-righteous friends and family if they can become humbly open-minded. My dad and my brother meant well; I will choose to believe their words were motivated by their love for me, however unwise and hurtful. They did not plan a negative outcome.

Most importantly, I have learned that I am the one who sets the boundaries of what I will accept from others, whether consciously or unconsciously. I "telegraph" my boundaries to those around me by my behavior, attitude, and confidence. I teach people how to treat me by what I accept from them! I teach others what I need from them. I teach them to respect me by respecting myself.

Have you ever noticed that confident, self-assured people don't go around whining about what to do, asking friends what to do, nor do they agonize over what they have already done? I used to do all that stuff! It signaled to my friends and family that, when it came to certain areas of my life, I had no confidence at all in my own decision-making ability.

I allowed my dad's advice-after-the-fact to further undermine my confidence. That was NOT his problem nor his fault. I could not change him; I did tell him once that some of his dry humor at my expense was hurtful, and he was surprised. He did not realize it affected me that way, and he immediately promised he would stop. He did. When Brother "Oughta," on the other hand, tries to tell me what I ought to do about various issues, I have learned how to respond in a way that he can understand means back off – with humor and self-confidence, even if I have to fake my confidence!

Other people's opinions of what I have done, am doing, or will do in the future are none of my concern and frankly, none of my business. All I can control, however, is my side of that. I call it what it is – none of my concern – and I keep my mouth shut. If they try to force a response, I still have options for possible ways to avoid unpleasant confrontation. Al-Anon teaches me short, polite scripted responses to use, such as "You may be right," or "I will have to think about that" and others. People are free to express their opinions about me or not, give me [unwanted] advice or not – I cannot control any of that.

All I can control is my response. And my response will always be some form of "back off, you're trespassing."

Another idea that struck me recently is this: when some people give me unwanted, unsolicited advice, it is usually something in THEIR own best interest. They want me to do something that will please them. I need to examine it closely asking myself, how is this to their advantage, and then asking, is it in my own best interest?

Once again, I need to make decisions that are good for ME and not give much consideration to its effect on others.

Mind Your Own Beeswax!

The serenity prayer asks for courage to change what I can, the ability to accept what I cannot change, and the wisdom to know the difference. Simply said, mind your own business and stay out of mine.

It sounds harsh, almost rude. The book of Thessalonians [4:11] in the Bible makes it clear: Mind your own business. And it says it just like that. There are good reasons for doing so. The Amplified Bible says to "make it your ambition and definitely endeavor to live quietly and peacefully, to mind your own affairs . . . so you may gain the respect of the outside world . . ."

The hardest part seems to be figuring out what is and is not my business. I remember teaching this passage in a women's Bible class in church. It was the most difficult lesson I ever taught. Those ladies were good women, loving, generous, kind-hearted, and hard-working. It was offensive to them to be told to mind their own business, but more so when I began to suggest that their adult alcoholic children, grown men and women, were none of these ladies' business ... I came close to being stoned!

It seems our children are highly valued "possessions" to some of us, not just on loan to train, discipline, teach, AND send on their way. As parents of small children, of course, we are totally responsible for their care, but at 30 or 45? Adult children who are not taking care of their own needs, depending on their parents for everything? What will happen to these "children" if and when you the parent dies? A major part of our parenting job is to enable them to leave the nest and live independently, successfully.

Of course, it is OK to help anyone who is having temporary difficulty. As an adult, I went home to my parents three times – for my own safety and my son's safety. It was not fun, but I was able to get employment and my own home. It felt awful to need assistance, but it was necessary. Thank God for family!

Had I stayed there, however, sitting on my dad's couch watching TV and expecting him, or worse yet, allowing him to be responsible for me as he had been when I was a child, it would have been the worst thing we both could have done.

My business is everything about me, inside out. Your business is everything about you, inside out. The only thing I can and should change is "ME, MYSELF, and I." The beauty of the serenity prayer is that it applies equally to each one of us wherever we are, because we each have different issues, flaws, needs, and defects. We are each at different points on our journey, the process of progress. I will change TODAY only what I learn needs to change, and accept TODAY only what I realize I cannot change . . . TODAY.

Accepting what I cannot change is very tricky for some people. It goes against my grain! I like to think I am a mover and shaker, an "agent of change for the better" wherever I go. My career as a teacher was all about molding and shaping and teaching and guiding others. My whole purpose as a parent was to raise a child to become everything he could be. What do you mean mind my own business?

My business I have determined so far is the following:

My attitudes, my beliefs, my opinions, my actions, my character defects, my happiness, my emotions, my thoughts, my feelings, my responses, my reactions, my word, my promises, my standards, my boundaries, my choices, my decisions, my motives, my personal care, my spiritual life, my relationship with God . . .

Did you notice one key word? MY.

Now notice this partial list of what is NOT my business:

What other people think of me, who likes me or not, why people do what they do and say what they say, how other people behave . . . You see, if there is anyone else involved, it is usually not my business.

It is my business to treat them well, but how they receive or accept that treatment is still out of my control and none of my business.

I can only do the next right thing. I can only do what I CAN do, and that's ALL I CAN do. I can be a good example, walking the talk, and sharing the message by talking the talk, but the results are none of my business. How can I control anyone else? With ropes and pistols like in the Wild West? Of course not!

I am not "responsible for" and I am not "accountable to God for" anyone but myself.

Someone said, "I am not my brother's keeper – I am my brother's brother." We are equals, and as such, we need to take care of ourselves as we walk alongside our brothers, being a good example, not goading, pushing, or pulling them! We can care, we can pray, we can empathize, we can help with basic needs, we can even bless with gifts, but we cannot "fix" what only God can fix. The best way to help someone else is to be a good example.

Even God does not treat us as badly as we treat each other. HE does not force His will on us; HE does not make us do anything; HE allows us to choose. He motivates us to do so with unconditional love and acceptance, with reminders of how good it will be FOR US to live according to His plan. The Bible uses language like choose, let, and allow when talking about the areas that are in our control.

Minding my own business is a lifelong, no-retirement full-time job, with great benefits, challenging enough!

"Mmmm . . . NOT Good!"

Campbell's soup is delicious! My favorite is the old stand-by, tomato soup. I love warm tomato soup in a large ceramic mug with buttery grilled cheese, a large slice of dill pickle on the side, and a glass of cold milk. A perfect winter lunch, comfort food, easy to make, and inexpensive. Mmmm – good!

How easy it is to fall into the following four m's that are not so yummy:

Martyrdom – look what I have done for that man/woman/child/friend, but look how poorly he repays me. Sounds like a prescription for divorce, or at least separation. Not so. Martyrs actually love it. They love feeling like a victim, unappreciated but essential to someone's existence. "Sigh. I break my back, I have to do everything, if I didn't do it, it wouldn't get done. Maybe it would get done but not done right [because I am also a perfectionist]." That seems to be the root of the martyrdom defect; it has to be done my way.

Controlling perfectionists get to do ALL the work because they insist! They love to complain about having to do it all, but they cannot delegate responsibility and trust others to do it "right" – which means their way. Martyrs are also borderline self-haters who love being persecuted, mistreated, or victimized by that "mean old alcoholic."

Manipulation – it's "what you have to do to get others to do what is best for them." This can be an insidious character defect, well-practiced and therefore perfected with much use. It almost seems the manipulator is unaware of doing it. In my experience, that's what happened. I whined, preached, discussed, threatened, nagged, debated, and cried. When the obvious methods did not work, I used calmer reason and quiet logic, appeals to morality and ethics. When that didn't work, I pulled out the big guns; I used my "feminine attributes" as collateral to get my way.

Manipulation is another word for game-playing, typical of children in junior high, but not mature adult behavior. The martyr is a great manipulator using tears, self-pity, self-blame, even self-hurt. A red flag about manipulation is this: if you say something once, it is stating a fact, request, or question; if you keep saying the same thing over and over, you are attempting to control the other person's response.

Mothering – loving them to death! This one is so hard to convince women of its negativity, even some men.

Because we were codependent, still attached at the umbilical cord, and had a distorted view of what love meant, we loved people to death. Literally. A handicapped adult, whether mentally or physically, needs help. That's expected and right and good.

A "healthy" adult – one who has the CAPACITY to be self-sufficient and independent – ought to be allowed the dignity of doing so, even if they do it less well than I may do it. Criticism, condemnation, judgment – these are forms of belittling and discouragement which never inspire anyone. Fear motivates temporarily - in prison camps! Oh, that God would set all the captives free, even those who don't know they are in bondage!

Managing is related to mothering; it means I act as their alarm clock, their calendar, their valet, their administrative assistant - their constant reminder of what they need to do to take care of themselves. I'm not doing it "for" them; I just feel the need to constantly "make sure" they do it. It is demeaning, humiliating, discouraging, and degrading. It sends a message to a capable adult that he is NOT really fully capable of taking care of himself.

A former friend, a capable adult and teacher, used to have her mother call her every morning, even in college. As teachers and friends, she roped me into calling her until I realized she was making ME accountable to the principal for both of us being on time or not. I quit being her alarm clock, and surprisingly, she managed to wake up on time.

I have done it all, and oh my, it was not good. I was a self-neglecting martyr who tried to mother, manipulate, and manage others while my own life was out of control – I was indeed powerless in their lives but unable to manage my own. That is true insanity.

Momentum Needs Failure

I was stuck! I depressed the accelerator, revved the engine, and I went only deeper into the mud. I sat. What to do?

I recalled my dad telling me to "rock" the car, putting it into "Drive" and "Reverse" alternately, each in turn, quickly as possible. The "backward, forward, backward, forward" motion would eventually build momentum, and the car would be propelled forward out of the rut, he said.

It worked.

It would not have worked without both slightly forward and slightly backward movement. Momentum needs the "failure" of backward movement.

This idea works for me in many areas of my life. It seems that in weight loss it is especially crucial. Thinking in terms of the backward movement of gaining a couple of pounds as building momentum is helpful in dispelling that discouraged feeling. Does it really help you lose more weight to gain a few? Of course not, but if you beat yourself up about one failure, you will be either moving backwards permanently or remain stuck where you are. Forward motion needs the "run and go" of backward movement to build momentum.

This is true in relationships. A guy calls every day for weeks, and then doesn't call for three days. The way you handle that "backward motion" will be important. If he never calls again, so be it. But if he does call after three days of silence, your positive acceptance of those days of silence will perhaps make your relationship really work. What guy wants to be scolded when he finally decides he really DOES like you – a lot – and calls to say so? Maybe his silence was simply time he needed to think. Your acceptance of that will be hugely important. Your scolding sounds like a shrew, whining sounds like a child, anger sounds like a bully, but acceptance ... it's what a confident lady does. "You can call me or not call me because I am fine with you or without you. I prefer with you, but I'm fine without you, too." I don't know about you, but that attitude would attract me if I were a man. Who wants to encourage a relationship with a shrew, a childish woman, or a bully? Not a real man, that's for sure.

Grown up men want grown up confident women. What may have appeared to be backward movement – not calling you – is your opportunity to practice confident acceptance and perhaps make real forward progress in the relationship, and if not, then at least progress toward building your own character.

Momentum is effective thinking to break a bad habit. Sometimes a few "failures" help you become determined to do better, to change your approach, to try something new IF you think of it positively as building momentum. I remember an AA friend of my family telling me not to be too disappointed if my newly sober son had some setbacks; in other words, if he drank again. He didn't, but I was ready to accept that possibility with a positive attitude. What if I had been treated like a failure every time I gained a couple pounds on my weight loss program? I would have given up ... oh yes, that's exactly what I often did!

Attitude IS everything. The perspective of seeing "failure" as building something good instead of as defeat makes a world of difference. If I can remember that in dealing with my alcoholic, I will have compassion for his struggle and keep a positive attitude toward my own.

Making mistakes in life is the same as making progress in getting out of a rut. It takes some backward energy or movement to move forward sometimes. Viewing my mistakes as "momentum builders" will help me deal with my imperfections. After all, only Jesus was a 100% perfect man ... and they crucified Him! It took the seemingly "backward" movement of apparent failure to achieve the ultimate miracle of His resurrection – without His death, there could be no rebirth. And without the hope of rebirth, we have only this life.

Failure is not failure until we quit trying to make progress. Mistakes are only building momentum for the future progress in life.

MY Happiness Is None of Your Business!

Codependency isn't really loving.

We think it is. We think it is the greatest kind of loving. As a well-meaning, loving friend or family member I have said, "When you're happy, I'm happy. When you're sad, I'm sad." And I want them to love me back for my desire to love them so fully.

However, that kind of "love" is not simply a kind of empathy. It's as if we are joined at the hip. I CAN'T be happy unless you're happy, and I CAN'T be happy unless we're together. I HAVE to see you, talk to you, know ALL about you. I don't want to share your life; I want to BE your life; I want you to BE my life. I want to be the most important thing IN your life. Period. It's as if we are not two people, but we are enmeshed, entwined like a vine twisting around a tree, with each other! This is not even biblical oneness which God desires for married couples. It chokes, controls, drains, and finally repulses us!

It is a possessive obsession, and that's NOT love.

Grown-up love, mature love, real love – whatever you want to call it - encourages self-determination and independence. As the saying goes so truly, "Love sets the beloved free."

Real love for your parents, siblings, boyfriend, girlfriend, spouse, or children is not possessive. It really does set them free, cliché or not. Real love has pure motives for the good of the other person, not for your own happiness. Real love is more interested in their happiness than your own. [Stop short of martyrdom, please. THAT can be the other extreme.]

1 Corinthians 13:4-8a says, "[PERFECT] love suffers long; is kind; does not envy; does not parade itself; is not arrogant; is not rude; does not seek its own; is not provoked; thinks no evil; does not rejoice in iniquity; rejoices in the truth; bears all things; believes all things; hopes all things; endures all things; never fails or vanishes. It is the greatest of the three – faith, hope, love."

But God is the only One who can love perfectly; this is a high standard, the basis of the principle I follow, but it is not possible for me to do perfectly. I am a human being, not a god-like creature. I need to allow GOD to love that other person perfectly – perhaps through me or not, but only God can.

Real love encourages me to have a life of my own, not to lose it in you. Real love encourages me to be me, not to change to suit you. Real love accepts me as I am. It empowers me to grow and change, if I want to, in whatever ways I want to change. Real love says you inspire me, you "make me want to be a better person," not FOR you, not to please you, but to improve myself because your love empowers ME to love ME also. It is freeing and encouraging and lifting. Real love gives me wings, not weights.

I have learned another thing about love – a very difficult thing. While it is ideal to be in a mutually loving relationship, no human relationship can possibly be equally loving. I have no control over a man's feelings. He has no control over mine. Some days I may FEEL great love for him, while he may barely like me. Other times it may be just the reverse. He may not feel "in love" with me but still be in a committed love relationship with me. My emotional response to him may be slight. Why? Any number of reasons can affect our feelings. The key thing is that we have decided – by an act of our wills – to be committed to each other in a loving relationship, with all its ups and downs, its responsibility, compromise, and adventure.

Is it really my responsibility to alleviate all of my adult loved one's suffering, discomfort, unhappiness, discontent, or negative consequences? Someone has said, "Pain is inevitable in life; suffering is a choice." Whose responsibility is it to make that choice? The answer is obvious to me now; it was not always so. It is MY choice to suffer or not. It is MY responsibility to alleviate MY own mental discomfort or unhappiness. It is my loved one's responsibility to alleviate his own unhappiness, too. My adult loved one's happiness is none of my business. Yes, while I desire to contribute to his happiness – we call it "making him happy" – I am not and cannot be the one held accountable for his happiness.

We are each accountable to God for the quality of our own lives. Jesus [my Higher Power] said in John 10:10, "I have come that you might have life, and that more abundantly."

God has set before me a banquet of happy choices, none of them immoral or illegal, and I have too long chosen to eat the crumbs. I can choose to be comfortable, contented, happy, satisfied, peaceful, and I can choose, in the middle of pain, not to suffer.

I remember an elderly woman at my mom's church who had had both legs amputated. When she was finally able to come to church in a wheelchair, I was amazed at how happy – downright joyful – she was! "How could she be happy at all with no legs?" was my thought. She made a choice not to focus on her losses but to focus on her blessings – she was alive, she was with her friends, and she knew God loved her.

Why do we choose to suffer when we can choose otherwise? Pain is still there, the past is done, mistakes have been made, and decisions must be accepted. What's done is done. Continuing to suffer over it is optional.

I choose love and peace. I choose serenity. As Robert Frost said in one poem, "You come too."

My Own BFF – ME!

I have had four best friends since childhood – my BFF's – Betty, Brenda, Carol, and Rosalee – [in alphabetical order, ladies]. We are all different – top-heavy, bottom-heavy, totally heavy, somewhat heavy, and not at all heavy; short, medium, tall; red-haired, blond-haired, gray-haired, white-haired, dyed-haired; nurses, teachers, postal workers; retired, not yet retired, no chance of retirement; blue eyes, brown eyes, green eyes; grandkids, no grandkids. We all wear glasses, believe in Jesus Christ as God, and have kids; four kids, one kid, two kids. We have all had long marriages. We've been single, happily married, unhappily divorced, and widowed. That's probably all they will allow me to say.

We are all crazy to some degree; one has papers to prove it, she would say; one is only slightly crazy when she's with the rest of us, we would say. We have all had life come at us hard. We have all kept a sense of humor and our faith in God, and very importantly, our friendship. There were times when we went our separate ways, but we could always take up right where we left off.

Since we have all passed the 60 mark, we make an effort to get together often.

I've been trying to figure out the glue which has held us together all these years. We have much more in common than I have mentioned, but nothing unusual. I think it's the fact that we all know the dirt on each other, and we still love each other; we accept each other – just as we are, with boatloads of baggage. We don't have to explain ourselves. We just know each other's stuff – our backgrounds, our parents, our educations, our problems, our struggles. We just know ... and we accept it! We have seen each other through horrible tragedies and cried in each other's arms; we have laughed hysterically together in the good times. Through it all, we have simply loved each other.

Why can't I be that much of a friend to myself? I am finally learning to do that. I am accepting "me" as I am right now, today. I am accepting all the "dirt" in my life, my past failures, mistakes, and sins. I am trying to unpack the baggage and travel light. As one friend says, I am trying to keep short accounts.

I have made some good decisions. I want to be deliriously happy on my last day. What if today is that day? Then I have to choose to BE that happy now. I cannot wait for my circumstances, my relationships, my finances, or God help me, my body to be perfect ... they will never be perfect in this life. I am only in control of MY happiness, MY attitude, MY thinking.

My teenage grand-daughter has a dozen smiley faces on her ipod, all white faces frowning but with one bright yellow face, smiling widely. She is the one smiling. "Everyone else can be miserable if they want to be, but I am going to be happy!" What a wonderful attitude! I want to be more like her when I grow up!

My Terrifying Secrets Everyone Already Knew

I thought I was fooling them. I thought no one else knew my secrets. I was terrified that I would be found out. It was a constant source of anxiety. "We are only as sick as our secrets," says an AA friend.

Then I went to Al-Anon, and there I thought everyone was supposed to be "anonymous" so I decided to use my middle name. More distorted thinking ... no, just plain nutty thinking. Get this: I thought that, if I saw someone who knew me at the meeting, it would throw them off if they heard me say my middle name, and not my first name. Now is that nutty, or what? I have a unique look. Anyone who knows me even slightly would not be fooled by a different name! OK, maybe if they haven't seen me in fifty years?

I misunderstood that the tradition was not being anonymous, or disguised, but of protected anonymity;

only what I reveal of my identity is known and only known
in the meeting by those present. We traditionally use only
first names, or whatever name I choose to use! I may
choose to reveal my full name, address, and all kinds of
personal information, but that information, my
anonymity, will be guarded just as you want yours to be
protected. "What you say here, whom you see here, when
you leave here, let it stay here." I can be assured that my
"story" will not become front page news tomorrow ... or
ever ... unless I am the one who publishes it.

I came to Al-Anon fearfully looking about,
wondering how it would affect my church family and my
extended family, but I was so miserable and so ready to
find relief that I didn't really care. I would deal with the
repercussions later. I came, fearful of speaking, because I
just knew they would think MY problems were so unique
and so strange that someone would say to me, "Honey, you
don't belong here. You need professional help." I was
prepared for that one; I already had an appointment the
next week for professional counseling! I came, fearful of
telling too much, fearful of crying in front of everyone,
and fearful of being judged because I wanted out of my
marriage of thirty years. Nevertheless, I came, fear and
all.

None of my fears happened. Isn't that usually the way
it is?

I did cry a little and say some things I know better
than to say now, but no one really seemed to mind. And as

I listened to others, I discovered kindred spirits in people of different status, different ages, genders, races, nationalities, cultures, religions, and professions. And from those kindred spirits I heard slightly differing versions of my own "story." There is tremendous understanding, patience, and love in those rooms both for the families and for the alcoholics.

I still held back some secrets.

I thought I needed to develop "trust" in these people. I usually trust people too soon too much. What I really needed was to become humble enough to open up about ME.

It is easy to go on and on about the alcoholic. We are experts at that, born of days, even years, of experience! Al-Anon is not a dumping ground for all our complaints about the alcoholic! It is a place to find serenity in spite of their alcoholism. And that requires humility.

Humility has no secrets. One saying in AA is, "We are only as sick as our secrets." I was very sick; I am getting well now. The prognosis is up to me. The treatment is up to me, self-prescribed, suggested only by others who were sicker than I am.

Al-Anon is not a group confessional. There is not one person who will tell you what to do about it. Just suggestions – keep coming back, read the Conference Approved Literature, get a sponsor and use the phone list, pray, meditate, etc. That's it. In fact, if you want to stay sick, you may choose to do so. You make the choices – all of them.

What were my secrets? You already know them because they may be your secrets, too:

1. I am not who or what you think I am. I am someone different than the public persona.
2. I am not as capable or smart or talented or competent as you think. I am more or less so.
3. I was a fraud, pretending that my life was good. Most of the time I was miserable.
4. There were many demons, fears, anxieties, sins, and much guilt inside of me.
5. I seemed like a sweet calm person. Inside I was often full of anger – unrecognized, unreleased, uncomfortable anger.

I believe the real "secrets to success" in life using **AA** and Al-Anon principles are the following:

Humility is essentially the first and continuous element. Without it I am stuck. Gratitude is the evidence of humility.

Trust, in my Higher Power and in myself, is a by-product of humility.

Acceptance at this very moment - of myself, of things, of people, and of current circumstances - is the key to serenity.

Seeing reality and truth help me find serenity here and now, not just as some faraway goal down the road.

Refusing to be a self-righteous judge of others is essential to maintaining humility, gratitude, acceptance, and trust in God. Only God has the knowledge required to judge others.

Humility, truthfulness, courage, faith – these are the tools we can use to cut out those awful, painful secrets – which everyone already knows! Are your secrets similar to mine?

The fourth step in twelve step programs is to take a fearless and thorough moral inventory of yourself, and in step five, confessing these character defects to yourself, God, and one other person. Steps 4 – 9 are essential, the summit to reach in order to find serenity [and sobriety] just over the horizon. This is the crux of the program: honesty, humility, willingness, open-mindedness, confession, and acceptance. We have been accustomed to being dishonest, arrogant, stubborn, narrow-minded, secretive, and judgmental!

OCD – Options, Choices, Decisions?

Options, choices, and decisions – if that's what OCD stands for, we all have it. Actually I may be deficient in it because I hate making decisions. Menus in restaurants used to drive me crazy. There are salads, sandwiches, pastas, seafood, chicken, beef, or I could have breakfast because they serve it all day. Social decisions baffled me. Should I go to the movies with my work colleagues or out to eat with my church friends? Financial concerns made me nervous. I can have one new dress, or two new pairs of shoes and a purse on sale, or a new coat if I use my discount card and a gift card which I had saved from my birthday – but which one to choose because I can't have it all unless, of course, I use my credit card!

I know. OCD actually means obsessive compulsive disorder. When I announced to my adult son that I am a bit OCD, he freaked out! "Mom, you don't wash your hands ten times a day!" His idea of OCD was the extreme socially unacceptable one; I am socially, acceptably OCD.

We call it being well-organized, detail-oriented, and thorough. Yep. I am all that – OCD - an Obsessed Control Diva with too many Options, Choices, and Decisions!

My OCD worked for me, most of the time, in my career and in being a decent homemaker. Organized classroom, organized house, organized car, organized purse. I organized my household chores using 3x5 cards from a book called <u>Frazzled Home Executives</u>. It really worked for me. I did the time study to see how long it actually took me, down to the minute, to do each household chore – washing dishes, with or without a dishwasher, vacuuming each room, dusting, etc. I also had to include every chore's frequency – daily, weekly, monthly, bi-monthly, quarterly, or yearly. [I actually used the system! Eventually its purpose is to free you of needing the system.]

At this point, you already know whether you are a fellow OCD sufferer, or you are living with one. There is hope either way.

Perfectionists all, that's what we are. Crumbs on the countertop, a wrinkle in the tablecloth, a smudge, a picture askew, a disorderly stack of books – these were of nearly life-and-death importance. The Al-Anon slogan "how important is it" does not work well for perfectionists with OCD. Everything is important to us!!

We had to learn how to prioritize, how to separate real needs and feelings from the "need for things to be in their place." I grew up with the old adage: "a place for everything and everything in its place." Not a bad idea, really, but in its place 24/7? When do you USE it? Could the pile on the floor be its place for NOW? My son is a neatly organized person, but as a teen, he used what he called the pile system! It drove me nuts.

As a former perfectionist and recovering OCD sufferer, I love the idea of "principles" instead of rules. Rules are like oak trees – they are domineering and unmoving and strong-looking, but let a hurricane wind come along and it will topple, roots upward. Principles are like palm trees – tall and quite noticeable and strong-looking, but let a hurricane wind come along and it simply bends over nearly to the ground before it succumbs to the wind. It stays rooted. I like roots to stay where they belong – underground.

I am learning to be a palm tree, not so much of an oak. I need to bend sometimes when a tough time assails my life. I used to believe I should be like the solid oak, standing firm and immovable to withstand the assault. It may work for others; I don't want to judge them, but I need to bend more. There just aren't as many beliefs, opinions, or preferences that should be set in concrete for me.

One pastor wisely taught me that there are three kinds of beliefs:

1. Doctrines – define a specific system of belief, a denomination; usually concrete issues.

2. Traditions – these give identity to a religious organization; somewhat flexible with group agreement.
3. Preferences – styles of music, times of meetings, length of meetings; very fluid.

The beauty of AA and Al-Anon is that their Twelve Steps, Twelve Traditions, and Concepts are universally accepted "doctrines," requiring the "group conscience" to keep the group's "traditions" identified as AA or Al-Anon; groups may function very well with meetings chaired by individuals with slightly different "preferences." Preferences should be the areas in which we bend; most often these are the causes of group disputes or church splits!

People with true OCD are not good at bending; they are rather inflexible. They are characterized by extremes in behavior, in language, and particularly in their thinking. My compulsive obsession focused on changing other people, things which were none of my business. I thought I was put on the planet to be a mover and shaker, an agent of change, divinely placed there to bring improvement, to make things better. Not totally wrong or bad, but the ways in which I implemented my alleged life's purpose could not have been worse.

The world needs movers and shakers, inventors, idea people, think tanks . . . perhaps in business and government, but not in other people's lives! My Options,

Choices, and Decisions are just that – MINE, and I need to let other people have their own choices as well, without judgment or criticism. I need to stop being an Obsessed Control Diva and accept the options, choices, and decisions that others make ... as well the ones I made in the past.

One Day at a Time, Sweet Jesus!

"One day at a time, sweet Jesus, it's all I'm asking of you ..." is a wonderfully simple, plaintive song. I like the version sung by Cristy Lane. She has a beautiful voice. I even sang the song myself in church. I just didn't have a clue how to apply its incredible truth to my own life until I came to Al-Anon.

It says "yesterday's gone and tomorrow may never be mine" but I held on to both "days" with all my emotional energy. I was pretty good at letting go of my past, I thought. I burned my bridges behind me . . . actually I blew them up with hand grenades! The rubble was what I still walked through. Tomorrow was an even bigger problem for me. Worry, fear, hopes, dreams, plans and schemes were the stuff of tomorrow.

I began meditating on Psalm 118:24 which says, "This is the day the Lord has made; we will rejoice and be glad in it." I paraphrased and personalized it: This is the day God has made just for me. I WILL be glad about it just as it is, with all its less than desirable circumstances, problems, and disappointments, and I WILL speak encouraging words, mind my own business, think positive thoughts, make decisions in my own best interest, accept what I cannot change, do the next right thing, and laugh out loud every chance I get, IN THIS day, all day long.

I have one prayer for each day - one prayer for myself and others – to know God's will and to have the power to carry it out. Thy will be done, O Lord, in my day, in my life, in the lives of everyone who crosses my path today.

Recently I made a transforming decision! I decided that I wanted to be "deliriously happy" on the last day of my life; I wanted to "end well." Then it occurred to me – what if today IS the last day of my life? Who knows? It might be. I have no guarantee of tomorrow. What am I going to do then to be deliriously happy today? NOW?

It transformed my life! I made a decision that, instead of seeing a day as part of a calendar of days, weeks, months, and years, I will see a day. Nothing more or less. One twenty-four hour period. I live like it is Groundhog's Day – remember the movie with Bill Murray? EVERY day is my one chance to be the best person I can be ... to improve my health, adjust my attitude, control my finances, change my habits, and strengthen my relationships if necessary ... just for today! There is no other day.

At the end of the day my prayer is to thank God for everything that happened today because I can assume that it was exactly what God wanted to happen in my life either for a lesson or a blessing. I asked for His will to be done. I believe it was done. Was it MY will? Not really, but He is God and I am not.

He knows what is in my best interest all the time. He sees the future, He knows all about the past. He knows me inside and out, my thoughts and feelings, my words spoken and unspoken. He knows my needs, and I trust that it is in His will to give me what I need. I do not always like the way He does that, but who am I to second-guess God? As God questioned Job, "Where were you when I laid the foundations of the earth?" Huh? Not there? All right, are we agreed that God is God and you are not a god-like creature?

I have one day, one 24-hour period of time . . . maybe. It could end early. I could die before midnight! I have to make every minute, every hour, every day count AS I AM LIVING IT. I used to put off my life until "someday," until next month, next weekend . . . tomorrow! When I get my debts paid off, when I lose weight, when I get time, when I get "around to it." I was good about meeting deadlines for projects; I hated leaving unfinished projects. I put off the things that were all about taking care of ME -- my health, developing relationships, being good to myself, and making my dreams come true.

I put off being really happy. I couldn't be happy since my circumstances were still imperfect. We used to live in a cute brick ranch – a "dollhouse" the realtor's description said – in Texas. Plano, Texas, is an upper middle class bedroom community north of Dallas. It is a beautiful city with excellent schools, parks, churches, restaurants, and shopping. It is divided into two sides of town, cut in two, not by a railroad, but by the expressway.

There is an east side and a west side; the west side is more desirable although, when I moved back up north, the east side was developing quickly with many homes in the seven-figure range. Not ours, of course. We were on the east side, just not the "right" side of the east side.

My house was everything I ever wanted, up to that point in my young life, except for a missing fireplace. This dollhouse had everything. It had three bedrooms, two full baths, a study, living room, roomy dining area, kitchen with dishwasher, garbage disposal, built-in oven and built-in range top – I loved it – a huge covered patio, attached two-and-a-half car garage with a door opener and a laundry area, a second parking driveway, a storage building, a nice fence, located on a corner, and with a curvy sidewalk up to the front door. But the part that sold me instantly was the "boy" bedroom – in white and blue with carpet that looked like jeans pockets and white built-in furniture perfect for my eight-year-old son! How could you beat that? It was my dream house (minus the fireplace).

This country girl finally had a brick ranch with air conditioning! I really thought God had answered all my prayers (except that part about the fireplace) because I had made a list before we went to Plano to look for a house, and my dollhouse had it all – (except the fireplace). It was not perfect. The decorating, except for the boy bedroom, was atrocious, but that was fine with me. I see myself as an amateur decorator, and it was full of potential.

Over the eight years we lived there, I transformed it on a very tight budget into a lovely home. It had one major flaw which I was unable to fix decoratively, however. The living room ceiling had a large crack coursing like a river across it. We were often invited to other couples' homes for dinner and other gatherings, but I was reluctant – just plain embarrassed – to invite them to our home ... because of that crack.

The crack. It was all I saw every time I walked into the living room. I just knew anyone who came there would also see only the crack. It was getting worse every day. I was becoming obsessed with it. I laugh now when I think about it. I was like the murderer in Edgar Allan Poe's story, "The Tell-tale Heart" in which he, the murderer, was the one who finally revealed his own deed because of his obsession with his own guilty beating heart. I was fixated on the flaw of that crack. I was the one who ultimately pointed it out to every visitor by apologizing for it and making excuses about why it wasn't repaired yet and how we were planning on getting around to it . . . someday. How foolish I was!

I had my dream house ... except for no fireplace. I had a beautifully decorated home . . . except for the crack. I lived in a beautiful city full of interesting people and fun things to do and places to go, but I always had to clean the house or grade papers or lose more weight or ... or . . . or try to be "perfect" before I could enjoy any of it. How could I, an imperfect woman, be "happy" with an imperfect house and imperfect circumstances?

Don't get a distorted idea that I was miserable all the time. I enjoyed my son, my job, my church, my friends, my decorating, and my house ... except for the you-know-whats.

I feel guilty sometimes for being so happy now – contentedly happy or belly-laughing happy – happy even when I was jobless, virtually penniless, and technically homeless living with family. I am learning to stay busy – thus this writing exercise. I am learning to take care of myself, to be good to myself; to enjoy my friends and to enjoy the simple things of life such as just walking together at the park. I am so rich in friends!

THIS is the day the Lord has made; I will rejoice and be glad IN it – now, today. "Let the weak say they are strong; let the poor say they are rich!" I AM strong; I AM rich! I have LIFE – I HAVE TODAY!

Cracks and fireplaces, be gone!

[P.S. I now have a cute little brick house WITH a fireplace and NO ceiling cracks! God is so good! And it helps to have an excellent landlord . . .]

A Penny's Worth of Progress

One penny added to another penny added to another penny . . . eventually equals a dollar. In this fast food world, I have seen people actually throw away pennies, not making the effort to pick one up to save.

It is this "instant coffee" thinking that has caused me so much grief in my own progress. I am a goal-oriented person, and I want to accomplish tasks, get things done. The idea of "never graduating" from Al-Anon was depressing and discouraging. I didn't want to think of possibly dying without experiencing complete recovery – finished, done, settled, all my plates spinning on their poles at one time. I was unhappy with slow progress.

I also used to be unsatisfied with cleaning only one room of my house a day. I used to be able to do a lot in one weekend. I could clean my two-story three-bedroom house and the basement playroom, where I carefully picked up every tiny little toy part. I did the laundry, washed my car, mowed the lawn, did the shopping, entertained friends on the weekend, sang in the choir, taught a Sunday School class, and was a single parent teaching full-time in public school. Everything in my house had to be in its place and clean. Unfinished projects bugged me. I loved to sew, but I would try to finish even a dress or coat in one day. It annoyed me to leave things unfinished.

That attitude worked well with jobs and chores. It doesn't work so well with character defects. Recovery, or experiencing daily serenity, is a process. We make progress, but we never reach perfection. That idea was very difficult for me to grasp, but as long as I could not get my thoughts centered on the idea of progress instead of reaching a final goal, I was exhausted and discouraged.

Finally an AA friend suggested that the peace I longed for could be found every day along the journey. I have to look for it, prepare for it, expect it, choose it, most of all, accept it. I also have to accept myself AS I AM TODAY, imperfect, whatever my circumstances, whatever my "everything" for today.

I am making progress one step at a time, like building a dollar one penny at a time. The peace I seek is available to me in exactly the quantity I need, just for today. Just like the Israelites as they traveled through the wilderness, God sent them manna – just exactly enough, never too little, never too much – but they had to believe it, accept it, gather it, and eat it in order to be nourished that one day.

Believe it! Accept it! Gather it! Consume it! I would do well to remember that in my pursuit of serenity. It is like daily manna – enough just for me, just for today if I read literature, attend meetings, and apply it with renewed thinking – consuming it!

Tomorrow I will need more; today's serenity will have been "consumed" already. In Lamentations, Jeremiah reminded himself that God's mercies are fresh every morning. His serenity is, too.

I can see my pennies growing into a dollar! In fact, I have begun a visible encourager – every day I put a penny into a Mason canning jar to see my progress. Imagine how much progress I will see in the jar in a year! I might even throw in some nickels, dimes, or quarters for especially "good" days.

What a treasure!

PMS = BS (Excuses or Reasons?)

I used every excuse, scheme, plot, and phony explanation I could to avoid situations I didn't like when I was younger. Sometimes my excuses were to myself, in my own head, just in case someone asked me why I was doing something they might think I should not be doing! Insanity at its best!

If I was supposed to be dieting [by my own choice], I would plan what I would say in case I was questioned at the check-out counter with Ho-Hos and chips in my cart ... "They are for my son's lunch," I would plan to say in reply. I have apparently been insane for a very long time ...

I always thought my feelings controlled me. I was helpless. I am woman! Hear me complain! I had premenstrual moods, postpartum blues; I was pre-menopausal, menopausal, and post-menopausal. I was controlled by my hormones. PMS became my favorite excuse for ... anything I needed an excuse for.

Even my female [former] OB-GYN told me in one visit that the cause of my complaints, which she did not even listen to fully, was that I was premenopausal. On the very next visit she scolded me for the same complaints because her prescription had not helped. She said, "Quit blaming your problems on menopause!" Hello! Who told me six months earlier that my problems were caused by menopause?

When my business partner and I decided to open an elementary school, I had the task of writing school policy. I loved it. Finally I was the one writing the "rules." When it came to our policy about lateness, I knew I would not have the time [nor the desire] to listen to tardy excuses every day. As the principal with no secretary, I was also teaching a multi-grade class. I had to have an efficient policy about tardiness.

I decided to give everyone in the school five excused times tardy each year, no questions asked. After that, every tardy was unexcused. I did not need [nor want] to listen to their REASONS for what they clearly had decided was a good EXCUSE for being late. I did not want to have to make a judgment call every day about the validity of their REASONS which they hoped would equal an EXCUSE. It worked well. Very few kids or their parents wanted to "waste" their excused times tardy. They did what they needed to do – got up earlier and left the house with plenty of time for just such unexpected events.

Reasons are just that – the cause of an event. Excuses have the connotation of making null and void the penalty for the negative outcome. Some reasons seem to have more validity because the reasons seem out of one's control. There was a long train; there was an accident; my son got sick at the last minute; a tree was down in the middle of the road, and we had to take a detour.

We seem to have been programmed to make excuses, to explain our actions, to look for a way out of the consequences, to avoid the penalty. Some people are experts at it. If only we could live in a world where there was no judgment!

There is and rightly must be accountability for our actions which result from our decisions. These days we have lost that concept as well. The Bible says in the days before the Judges that, because there was no king to force accountability and because people refused to accept accountability before God, "everyone did what was right in their own eyes." It was chaotic, of course. Refusing to accept accountability does not nullify the consequences; it only increases the chaos.

Reasons are just that – the factual, objective, unemotional cause of an action. Excuses never remove the consequences of the action; they are an attempt to invalidate the cause.

Now one of my mottos is ... "If you mess up, fess up!"

Practice Never Makes Perfect

Do you believe "practice makes perfect"? Or if at first you don't succeed, try try again? Forget it. You are human. You will never be perfect on this earth. Tiger Woods seemed like the perfect golfer. Michael Jordan seemed like the perfect basketball player. Both were ... until a better golfer or a better shooter came along, or until each of them just got older.

Who said anyone needs to be "perfect" anyway? Someone must have told me I needed to be "perfect" because I have been trying to "dream that impossible dream" all my life – unsuccessfully. It hurts. All that effort of striving, straining, reaching, grasping, and searching has not worked. I must have a deeply seated flaw that is hindering me from that goal. I need to try something else – another plan, another program, another place, another person, another job – that will help me be successful. All the ads on TV say their plan works when others don't. Their weight loss plan, their money plan, their hair care plan, their health plan, their political plan, their religious plan works – they may work for some people, but not for me. I am still terribly flawed.

I am never enough. I am just not good enough, skinny enough, rich enough, cute enough, smart enough, wise enough – I am not enough! But I am totally human, like everyone else, right? Why are others enough? Why am I told to give THEM a "pass" – to accept THEM – to "overlook" THEIR faults? When do I get a pass, have MY flaws overlooked, understood, accepted?

I have also been told lately that I have really changed a lot – for the better! Wow. I must have been one rotten person if a) I have changed for the better so much, and b) I am still not good enough! What utter despair to feel that I have indeed made progress on my character flaws but still not enough. My family all spent a lot of time and energy focused on my flaws, it seemed to me. And they still believe that "I have miles to go before I sleep." [Robert Frost]

Was all that meant to deflect me from seeing their flaws? Was it because looking at my flaws was like looking at themselves in a mirror? Was it because my flaws were somehow worse than theirs? Was it because my parents had given up on themselves and put all their hopes of perfection on me? "To analyze is to paralyze," they say in Al-Anon.

But this I know. I do NOT need to strive to really be perfect. A KJV Bible verse says, "Strive to be perfect."

Problem: perfect in KJV English means mature, not literally perfect. I do need to WANT to be mature. What does being perfect really mean? What does it look like in human form? It looks like my Higher Power – Jesus Christ – my God as I understand Him. He said we should strive to be "mature." MATURE – grown up, wise, self-assured, compassionate, understanding – mature; not IMMATURE – childish, foolish, insecure, self-centered, distorted. My efforts need to be aimed toward PROGRESS in the direction of wisdom, confidence, compassion, sane thinking, and chipping away daily at my character defects, one at a time, one day at a time, with the help of God.

Practice can keep things exactly the same! "Just keep doing what you have always done, and you will keep getting what you have always gotten." That's the definition of insanity! Practice never makes perfect; perfect is not attainable. That clever re-wording of the old adage -- "Perfect practice makes perfect" – actually creates more distorted thinking because there is no such thing as "perfect practice."

If Michael Jordan or Tiger Woods were ever truly "perfect," logic says they would still be perfect. Perfection has no end, no deterioration point, no decline. But it also cannot be replicated. Perfection's nature is that it stands above all others. It is the standard against which everything else is measured. Only God, as I understand

Him, is truly perfect; therefore, He alone is worthy of worship.

Why be concerned with worship? The very nature of our humanity is imperfection, on purpose. If any human being could attain any kind of perfection, we would then be able to sustain it. If we could sustain perfection, we would be worthy of worship, and would indeed be gods ourselves. Ever since the first humans we know about - Adam and Eve - we have all had one major flaw – this desire for, this striving for, this coveting of god-like perfection. Eve's downfall was that she believed the lie – "you shall be like God, knowing ..." Who cares what they would know. The point is they were captured by the desire to be gods – super-powerful, super-intelligent! There may not have been a literal apple; but there was a real lie they believed! The "sin" was arrogance, a prideful, stubborn, arrogant lack of humility, in my opinion.

I tease my brother, calling him a god-like creature because he says he "knows" things others don't know. [Actually he has the spiritual gift of discernment.] The truth is we all secretly (or openly) want to be these god-like creatures. The real original sin, or character defect as I prefer to say, was not disobedience of a rule. The real problem was pride, I believe.

The Bible is full of anecdotal praise for people who showed humility – the sinner who prayed, the poor widow who shared, the crippled man who waited – always the poor, the afflicted, the prisoner, the obvious sinner. God says He lifts up the humble; He draws near to the humble; He blesses the humble. I used to think, as some of you may think, that poor, simple, weak people were drawn to a belief in a deity because they were poor, simple, and weak. No, they are drawn to God because they are not competing with Him! They are not proud, self-centered, self-willed, or thirsting for power.

The first step in the Twelve Steps of AA and Al-Anon says, "We admitted we were powerless [over alcohol or whatever], and that our lives had become unmanageable." That required humility, admitting my own powerlessness and an inability to manage my own life. How low must I go? I am already powerless and I can't manage my own simple life? Then later I confessed my need for a Higher Power – better and more able than I – to restore me to sanity. I thought that was humiliation enough. Now I must confess my character defects. How utterly low did I have to go to find this peace I am looking for?

Talk about letting go of pride – confessing powerlessness, an inability to manage my own simple life, and now I confess I am extremely flawed – insane! There can be no pride left there. Powerless, unable to function maturely as an adult, and insane. No god-like creature here!

Perhaps that's why parents try to give their children "better" lives, more stuff, more opportunities. They realize their chance for "perfection" has passed, but they have a chance to be god-like as they raise these children. We mold and shape and nurture and guide and instruct our children so they will outstrip us, still striving for that perfection which only God possesses. We still try to control them because we are the "Parents" – the godlike creatures who know best. Remember the TV show of the fifties called "Father Knows Best"? Yes, Father knows best when children are very young, but if Father still thinks he knows best when his children are 45 years old, something is very wrong. That father must still be striving to be a god-like creature in his son's life.

One of the most damning character defects is the thirst for power. My brother calls it PMS – power, money, and scandal. They do seem to go together, those three. Rarely do we see men or women rise to great power or riches without scandal. Billy Graham, Cliff Barrows, and George Beverly Shea made a pact as very young men in the ministry to protect each other's reputations by being accountable to each other. It seems to have worked; all three men lived to be past 90 (Shea died at 103!) and they succeeded in staying morally free of scandal, a rare thing in Christian ministry. Accountability requires humility and honesty.

Only practice which increasingly moves "toward perfection" by continually improving on technique, attitude, methodology, strategy, or accuracy is beneficial. That's the "practice which makes progress." Aiming toward a high goal is a smart thing to do; expecting to reach it is not wise.

The movie "When the Game Stands Tall" is the true story of the winningest high school football coach in history. His motto was "perfect effort." I like that. Give it everything you have! Give your best effort and trust God for the results. Let's make our new motto "perfect effort makes good progress."

Priceless Peace!

What would you give to find the greatest thing on earth, something everyone else wanted, too?

The Bible illustrates truth with parables. There are things set apart, sanctified things which have greater value – the pearl of great price, the virtuous woman, the crown of glory, the holy items of the temple.

But the most priceless pearl is "the peace which passes understanding" – peace which seems to defy nature and logic and reason. Peace IN the middle of a storm, not afterwards when we realize we survived it. Peace during the sickness, hearing of the loss, during the tragedy, while the pain persists.

Peace that cannot be explained is priceless.

Everyone has a sense of relief – a form of peace – when circumstances are settled, when pain subsides, when mourning ceases. Few know peace in the middle of it all.

But peace can be yours any time.

Jesus knew all the problems and pain, all the trouble and temptations, all the grief and gut-wrenching unfaithfulness people can dish out. Yet He knew peace; He knew how to access peace, not just as God-in-the-flesh, but as a man – a human being. He was as human as we are.

Peace has many synonyms in the Bible: contentment, serenity, satisfaction, well-being, joyfulness. Peace basically means an absence of the feelings, thoughts, and desires which cause the opposite of peace, the things which make us discontent, uneasy, unsatisfied, joyless. It is not our circumstances which rob us of our peace; it's our thinking.

Romans 12:2 says to "be transformed by renewing your mind." That means to become more like Christ we must change the way we think. WE have to DO that. WE have to DO the WORK involved in changing our thinking.

"LET this mind be in you which was also in Christ Jesus..." LET means an act of our will, a choice we make. God is still a God of free will. He does not force us to do anything. He lays out the positive results and the negative consequences of our choices, but He never forces His will on anyone. He says He stands at the door and knocks, waiting to be let in; he does not beat it down!

Peace is a choice to have a different perspective. Look at the problem from the mountaintop, not the valley. Find a positive outcome.

I know the story of Pollyanna is considered a cliché, but it actually works in real life! Spread joy to others to be happy yourself!

Reese's Cups

One of my AA mentor friends used to tell me, "Be good to yourself." I liked that idea! I interpreted it to mean indulgences. In my family in the fifties, treats and desserts were only for special occasions. We never had soft drinks except for holidays or birthday parties. We had only water and milk, and Cool-Aid in the summer.

I also thought extravagance was "being good to myself." Extravagance to me meant "if one is good, more is better." Over-spending, buying two pairs of shoes instead of one, spending more than I could afford, was also considered "being good to myself." I had visions of fresh flowers delivered daily, getting pampered professionally, splurging on new outfits, spending money we didn't have [with those evil credit cards] for things we didn't need ... and Reese's cups.

Reese's cups were my favorite treat. I made sure my students and friends knew it. That way I would get some for my birthday, Christmas, Easter, Halloween, and the end of the school year. At least I hoped. But I also indulged when I needed to be comforted, to celebrate, to alleviate boredom, to express anger [How crazy is that?], to satisfy a craving!

Lately I started thinking about how other people are being good to themselves or not. My mom takes care of her body, exercises, chooses good food, but buys whatever new clothes she wants. My friend's goal is to "save a dollar on every transaction" and yet he buys expensive cigars and drives a Cadillac. One owns a Florida condo, but suffers pain exacerbated by cold northern winters. One friend buys all her clothes from resale shops, but eats out often.

I asked myself, how are these people being good to themselves? ARE they being good to themselves? We all deserve good treatment. What is a balanced approach, and what are the best priorities for ME?

I have decided what "good treatment" looks like. It may not be what you think good treatment is. That's fine. We all have issues from our lives that dictate our definition of good treatment. One old friend would not allow his wife to buy anything but pure white sheets because, he said, he spent too much time in WWII sleeping on dirty grey sheets. Experiences differ.

I realized I am my own best friend, greatly loved, honestly having my best interests at heart, so I made the following list of what "being good to my friend – [or to me] – " looks like:

Time, positive talk, and loving touch are my love languages. I express love for my friends by spending time with them, speaking encouragingly to them, and giving them hugs. Therefore, I will speak to myself positively, give a reasonable amount of daily time to my own care, and give myself virtual "hugs" when I need them. I will write myself encouraging notes on my kitchen blackboard and post-it notes on my computer. I will put positive sayings and biblical passages on 3x5 cards around my house.

Money is a big issue with my friends. They are mostly "savers" not "spenders." They are generous with others. Some won't even spend money on themselves. When I look at this issue, I have decided to pay cash for everything I can, staying on a budget to save for those items. I will "do without" whatever is not essential to my survival, but I will place my own health, safety, and security as top priorities. Secondly, I will be generous with myself in ways that promote my long-term goals of good health, fitness, and career success. Thirdly, where money is concerned, I will be as generous to others as possible because my friends generously helped me when I was in need. Finally, I can still have "champagne taste on beer money" by shopping creatively at resale shops and garage sales.

Being good to my friends means I feed them healthful foods, encourage their exercise programs, and compliment their progress. Therefore, I need to feed myself only healthful foods and encourage myself with positive self-talk about my progress. I need to take my medications, follow doctor's orders, get lab work, and take supplements suggested. I will spend money on healthful foods, not thinking of them as too expensive.

I taught driver's education to teenagers, but I have never liked wearing a seatbelt. Being good to myself means I will wear that seatbelt! I will take care of my car for safety's sake. I will practice what I preached!

I will make it a top priority to take time to look my best – to be well-groomed; get professional haircuts, dental work, eye exams, glasses. I will wear sunscreen and take care of my feet [as a diabetic]. I will look my best – light makeup, neat, clean, well-fitting clothes, comfortable shoes. I am worth it.

I want my friends to enjoy daily life, so I will see that I enjoy my daily life, today, now, in spite of circumstances. I will do and think and read and write whatever it takes. I will have relationships with people who are "energizers, encouragers, and empower-ers." I will tactfully back away from people who are energy vampires, discouragers, whiners, liars, abusers, and users.

Finally, I want to encourage my friends to grow, to learn, to gain wisdom, to become the unique individuals God planned them to become. Therefore, I will do something daily to grow spiritually, to learn something new, to improve a skill, to discover ME.

There are still Reese's cups on my "Christmas list," but I don't need to eat the whole package at one sitting.

THAT would not be good for me, I have finally decided. I am beginning to like the grown-up person I am becoming.

Shut Up and Listen, You Might Learn Something

"You're a born teacher," they said.

"It comes naturally," I said. "I can teach anybody anything if I can learn it first myself."

I am instructively helpful, the nicest kind of know-it-all. When I was a child, I even had a little pink diary which had inscribed on the cover: "Little Miss Know-It-All." Proof positive.

So when I came to Al-Anon, I came with the good intentions of being as instructive and helpful as possible. Of course, I came to learn as well. I did not intend to whine and complain about my husbands and their flaws; "I am only here to fix me," I confidently stated in one of my first meetings.

Meetings are designed for the most members to get maximum benefit. That means members take turns, speak briefly, and stick to issues regarding their own recovery, not the alcoholic. Imagine how unproductive meetings would be if everyone used it to bellyache about the other person's misconduct. Meetings do not necessarily have a "support group" mentality. There are too many people with too little time for everyone to gripe.

Newcomers are given an opportunity to speak if desired, and since they are new, they are given some leniency about time limits and topics. Most newcomers spend their entire time griping about the alcoholic. That attitude changes after a few meetings. A lot of what some people do in meetings should be done in private with a sponsor or on the phone, one on one. But Al-Anon is gentle to us.

One passage in one of our CAL books suggests that there is a happy medium between never speaking up and being a chatterbox. We need to listen to gain information, and we need to share our own experience, strength, and hope to be a help to others. It is always beneficial to me to listen intently, think deeply about the topic, and choose wisely what to say and when to say it.

Why is all this so important as to deserve a whole chapter? The issue of humility is the bedrock of success in AA and Al-Anon and as a Christian. Humility is essential, not optional. Other principles may take longer to develop, but progress rests on certain main pillars – the most important being humility.

But I didn't think I lacked humility. Yes, I have struggled with my body image all my life. I used to think

I was a social misfit, as well. But I have known I am "smart" since first grade when I was put in the "red bird" reading group. Good grades, awards, a college degree, and a 30-year teaching career have not changed my mind about that. So when it involves only my brain, I am confident.

If I have to coordinate my brain AND my body, things get shaky. Typing, for example, is one skill I have never mastered. I dropped speech class in high school because I was too shy and took a semester of typing instead. Somehow I passed with a B or C but I did not master correct finger placement and continue to look at the keys when I type. I am looking at them now! But I have never held a job requiring precise typing technique. I am accurate, but not technically correct. I don't really care.

Because I was not perfect at anything and had a poor body image, I thought I was humble. Not true at all! As long as I could be superior intellectually, I was not concerned. In fact, I rationalized that I didn't care about my imperfect body because I "had a brain." Like Dorothy's friends in "Wizard of Oz," I thought I just lacked one something. I compensated for the social skills I thought I lacked in other ways. I turned to my church, books, imagination, daydreams, and writing. As long as I stayed out of uncomfortable social situations with boys, I was all right, but I was never really very happy.

The problem with poor body image was in my head. I telegraphed to others that I was the one who thought something was wrong. In contrast, I exhibited confidence in the area of my intellect. To be fair, I was highly validated for my intellectual ability; I was rarely validated for my body. I was the butt of many family jokes related to my weight and my hair. It is still a sensitive subject. I wish my family and well-meaning friends would simply say hello rather than add a comment about my weight or my hair. Why can't people just say hello? Who gave them the right to evaluate me? [Oh yes, I did, unwittingly!]

Is this really about humility or listening? Yes, it is. It takes humility – actually meekness – to submit to the voices of others sharing their experience and their strength and their hope. It takes real listening – not just physically hearing – to grow in Al-Anon. Humility says my story is mine to share, but it is also the prerequisite for trust. It takes humility to share my own experience, strength and hope because pride would have me keep it to myself. I could think, "It's none of their business." Entering the rooms of AA and Al-Anon is an act which opens me up to their "business" as they share; likewise, when I share, I must trust them to keep my anonymity, not gossip, not judge, and not tell me what to do. It is an understood deal we make when we sit down in an AA or Al-Anon room.

When I shut up and listen, I can learn. When I shut up and listen, I allow others to share and learn. There are no "authorities" or "experts." We are equals, on a level plane with similar stories and similar problems as the result of the same disease -- alcoholism.

I need to have the humility to shut up and listen. I might learn something. Think of that!

Something There is that Doesn't Love a Wall

Robert Frost, my all-time favorite poet, wrote the poem "Mending Walls" shortly after the inauguration of President John F. Kennedy. This was at the time of the infamous wall dividing the city of Berlin between the Communist side (East Berlin) and the free side (West Berlin). I cannot imagine what it must have been like to be stuck living on the free half of a city which was in the middle of Communist East Germany. Free within the city, but not free to leave the city, not free to visit friends and relatives on the other side, not free to visit friends and family in the surrounding country of East Germany. Not free to visit free West Germany!

The poem is about two men, living on New England farms which share a beautiful loose stone wall between their properties, who, in New England tradition, are walking the wall on either side, picking up stones which have tumbled off, and replacing them. They carry on cordial conversation as they walk the wall, but they are essentially rebuilding a structure which divides them. The farmland of New England is terribly stony, so building the wall serves two purposes: clearing the land of the small boulders which inhibit farming and defining each other's property line. The neighbor in the poem boasts, "Good fences make good neighbors."

The Berlin wall finally came down during the Presidency of Ronald Reagan, after his speech in which he said the famous words, standing in front of the wall on the West side, "Mr. Gorbachev, tear down this wall!" You see, people living on the Communist side of the wall had been shot trying to escape. They could only leave the city with special permission from the government which involved lengthy waits and much red tape. The yearning of their hearts was to be free.

Walls set boundaries. Walls divide. Exterior walls protect us from predators and the effects of bad weather. Walls are built to be permanent, impervious to assault from without. Like the fable of the three little pigs, the smart pig built his house of brick and saved them all from the big bad wolf. What the smart pig's brothers did not consider was that his brick house might have been built to keep them out as well. Only in the emergency of the moment did he let them inside. Just a thought.

Walls built to protect me from people who might hurt me also left me lonely, isolated, and yearning for freedom much like those Berliners. And like them, I had no power to escape or to tear down the wall, I thought. It was a lie – more distorted thinking. I had ALL the power to tear down my walls. I built them, and I could tear them down. Fear helped me build them and fear kept them in place. I had to defeat fear before I felt safe enough to begin assailing the walls.

Walls are prominently discussed in the Bible. Nehemiah directed the rebuilding of the wall around the city of Jerusalem; the walls of the city of Jericho fell down after a weaponless march around the city for a week, once a day for six days and seven times straight on the seventh day. The walls crumbled. Walls were so thick in those days that houses could be built on top of them, so this was an ingenious strategy.

Part of the strategy of Jericho's defeat was to create fear in the residents. They had already heard of the reputation of the Israelites and their God. When the dreaded Israelites showed up in the neighborhood, fear increased. Watching from their high narrow windows on the wall, the first march around their city must have felt to the inhabitants like anticipating a terrorist attack; all the Israelites did was to march around them and return to their own camp.

After six days of this I imagine some of the residents of Jericho became somewhat complacent. "There they go again. When are those idiots going to stop their tramp-tramping around us?" Others might have become increasingly nervous, wondering what was going to happen next, and when – tomorrow, next week, when? Both were born of reactions to fear.

Some, I am certain, did not sit around waiting and wondering. They were proactive movers and shakers – I would have wanted to be one of these. They were organizing people, gathering weapons, sharpening spears, rallying citizens for a certain attack.

I remember my days of growing up in the sixties, the Cold War fears of "the bomb" being used against us. Bomb shelters were built deep underground with thick walls. Literature, movies, sermons, poems, art, and songs of the times reflected the fear of atomic war. Our parents had lived through World War II and were not eager for a third. Fear was ripe. I remember often wondering, as I walked the halls of high school, if I would even live to graduate. I was afraid of dying. I turned to God, but some classmates turned to drugs, alcohol and a hedonist attitude of "eat, drink, and be merry, for tomorrow you may die." Some of them did.

Fear is a powerful thing, and it is strong motivation. It is the mortar that builds many walls.

Walls can also create an atmosphere of mystery about what is hidden inside. There is an allure that can accompany such mystery. The contradiction of the protective purpose of the wall combined with curious attraction to the unknown behind the wall is the stuff of more fairy tales.

Rapunzel comes to mind. Who knows why she was imprisoned in that walled tower, but there she was. And how did the handsome prince, one of many who seemed to inhabit fairyland, know she was there? Oh yes, she appeared at the window occasionally with such beautiful long hair. The handsome prince gets the credit for her rescue, but if she had cut off her hair, how would he have saved her? Just another question I should have asked my fairy godmother.

Walls, therefore, seem to be a contradiction in themselves. Built to protect, they isolate. Built to fend off predators, they invite curiosity. Built by the residents themselves, they often imprison.

Is there someone who doesn't love a wall, Frost hints questioningly? I hold up my hand in reply, "Sir, with all due respect, me."

I am not for one minute suggesting that I would prefer living without them, but I am suggesting that perhaps I should rethink my wall-building activities. A collection of large, light-inviting windows scattered throughout the structure, with double doors located in highly accessible and inviting intervals in the wall would be more to my liking. I would love seeing light filtering through tall windows and views of nature's beauty as I walk through my imaginary home. Yes, my home will have walls for all the good reasons, but I will have windows and doors to let in beauty and welcome love.

So my house, the one I carry around with me – my body, soul, and spirit – must have some walls for protection, some windows for interacting with the world, and some inviting doors for relationships. Mr. Frost, I apologize. I think maybe walls do serve a purpose. Like the smart pig, I think I need to be able to recognize the enemy when I see him but not use walls to keep out the beauty of nature and the love of friends.

I am so excited! I want to build my dream house. I think maybe it needs movable walls because I don't want to exclude my loved ones; I want to invite them to be sheltered there but keep out enemies who would harm me. My dream house will have around it a boundary, a low wall made of stone; natural fieldstone is my favorite. The stones will not be cemented together; I may want to move the wall, closer or farther out. It needs to be somewhat flexible.

I love natural materials – wood, stone, brick, bamboo, rattan, wicker – the same stuff God uses to build His world. My dream house needs to be natural and real. It will include the colors of the sky and the earth, the textures of a lakeside. My dream house will have tall, wide windows; double doors that lock as needed but are inviting when desired.

It's my house; I alone hold the key. I designed it, built it, paid for it, and it is my responsibility to maintain it – remodeling it according to my needs.

What does all this talk of houses and walls really mean? My house is my LIFE -- my choices, my beliefs, my memories. I can create boundaries for protecting myself and move those boundaries any way I choose.

It's my house – my life. If you don't like my house – my boundaries - then try next door. Thanks, Mr. Frost.

Standards Are What I Stand On

Simple idea.

Standards I have set for myself, not for anyone else.

My choice of standards is my set of beliefs about what my words and my behavior ought to be, modified to fit my changing life's patterns, my experiences, and my beliefs formed and ever-changing over a lifetime.

Standards are not hard and fast rules, but something to aim for, an ultimate goal to reach. For example, I have a goal of weight loss. I have made progress; I have more to lose before I reach the ideal weight for my age and height. I do not beat myself up because I am not there yet; I applaud myself for progress. Likewise, some of my standards for my life are goals, some goals which are way out there may never be reached. They are MY goals, MY standards, just for ME. Standards are what I think – not what you think – is best and right for me.

Standards are what I choose for myself, not what you impose on me, nor what I may attempt to impose on you.

If I join a group – a church, a club, a political organization, a service group – I accept their requirements for membership until I decide that any one of those requirements is unacceptable. If they try to force their requirements on me or to impose their standards on me, they are acting like a cult. Cults are in Guyana and Waco and anywhere that we individuals are not truly free to be ourselves, to choose for ourselves.

My standards do not need anyone else's approval, validation, or confirmation. They are mine. I chose them; I created them. They may have their origins in a creed, a religious organization, or a book, but these standards are mine, not yours. You are free to adopt my standards, word for word, if you want them. I will not impose them on you, however. That would be like forcing you to wear my shoes, my size, worn down in my unique way. They will never really fit YOU.

My standards are all about my actions and my words. Below I have delineated my standards, and while there may be mention of other people, it is only with reference to how I treat them.

<u>My standards cannot include any attempt to control other people's behavior or words.</u>

Without attempting to impose my standards on you, my reader, let me illustrate:

I believe in privacy and discretion, especially regarding physical intimacy. We might hold hands, sit close with arms around each other, and even kiss hello or good-by in public, but that's the limit.

I believe in following the Ten Commandments to the best of my ability – the principles behind them, that is. For example, the first four are all about loving God with my whole heart, soul, mind and strength; the fifth is about honoring and respecting my own origins – my parents, my family, my culture, my roots; the last five are all about respecting the rights of others. My freedoms must not violate the well-being of others.

I believe in the serenity prayer – accepting the things I cannot change and changing only what I can. I believe in the Lord's Prayer as a model prayer.

I do not use the names of God and Jesus Christ in any way other than prayer, praise, or instruction. While I believe that Jesus is the one true God, I still believe in respecting others' rights to believe as they choose.

I hate all forms of bigotry, prejudice, racial discrimination, and ethnic stereotypes. I especially hate ridicule of mentally, emotionally, psychologically or physically handicapped people.

I dress modestly year round. I don't display my cleavage, my bare midriff, or my bare butt. I wear a minimum of makeup. These standards for my appearance make me feel comfortable. However, I may admire others who dress differently.

I believe in all the slogans, principles, steps, and traditions of AA and Al-Anon.

I believe in giving a full day's work for a full day's pay, being honest in all my dealings, and obeying the Law of the Land to the best of my ability.

This is not a comprehensive list of my standards, just examples. Standards guide my life like a compass.

When I judge you – decide whether you are right or wrong – for not following MY set of standards for YOUR life, I am placing myself above you in a superior position. I have no right to do that; we are on the same horizontal plane – equals as human beings. An employer, a school, a church, a government can require certain things from me, to which I agree in advance; but I may choose to leave the job, the school, the church, or even the country if and when their requirements are onerous. MY CHOICE! The leader of each of those entities has a certain authority delegated to them by appointment, election, or promotion. I still have a choice about submitting to them. What a wonderful country we live in which gives us such freedom of our wills! And best of all, what an awesome and gracious God Who allows us the same!

When I try to impose my standards on you or judge you as "wrong" for not following MY standards, I am not treating you as an equal human being. The problem with this arises with children and spouses. I have an equally agreed upon relationship [ideally] with my spouse. With my child, I have two relationships – one as parent while he is a child, and later as friend when he is an adult.

Some parents and adult children have a hard time with that role change – when does it actually change, how does it change, and why does it need to change? When my son was little, I literally imposed my standards on him and set consequences when he did not keep them. I told him what to wear, where he could go, when to come home, and even who his friends were ... as a preschooler. If I were still doing any of that now that my son is past 40, Houston, we would have a problem!

The problem occurs, in my experience, when I confuse my standards – just for ME – with my boundaries – just for YOU. The boundaries are my rules of engagement. I don't even have to tell you what they are. I may never tell you, but I will "telegraph" them to you by the behavior and words I accept from you. I also have the right to change my boundaries if I see that a relationship is changing – becoming unhealthy or becoming more serious. My choice, my boundary line. I have had problems with this principle because I sometimes allowed what should have been unacceptable behavior and words to be acceptable.

I teach others how to treat me by what I allow them to do or say ... TO me.

Another decision - to live up to my own standards or not - is still my choice.

I can change my standards any time I choose.

I am an independent adult woman.

Wow.

Still Parenting Your Adult Child?

This is such a sensitive issue that I need to express these ideas as compassionately as I can. I have a son – one terrific, intelligent, talented handsome guy – who has always been the "sunshine of my life." I would gladly give my life's blood, any organ, or the breath I breathe so that he could live.

But he is an adult now. How old is he? It doesn't matter. Some people become adults at 12, some at 21, some never do and then die of old age. An adult is defined, in my opinion, as "an independent self-sufficient person willing and able to make decisions and choices in his/her own best interest." Granted, not many of us are truly adults. That's just my point.

If parents could only make the really tough calls at those crucial moments in their kids' lives, their children would have a better chance of becoming true adults at a reasonably early age.

My son is perhaps more adult than I am. He is independent, self-sufficient, a good husband and father, a good provider, an excellent coach, making decisions and choices not only for himself but for his family WITHOUT MY INTERFERENCE. And if I offered unsolicited advice, he would quickly tell me to mind my own business. And I LOVE IT! Once I asked him if he had his priorities right, of course full of the judgment that I believed he did not. His response to me was profoundly perfect: "Mom, no they aren't, but all you need to do about it is to pray for me."

Was he always this mature? Did I do everything right? Has he never made any bad choices? For over three years, he made the bad choices I had warned him not to do. He made some poor decisions. He left home when I threw him out! It was the worst, hardest, and best thing I ever did because within ten months he was sober, right with God, making amends to me, and our relationship was restored.

That's the short version. It was painfully complicated. I made mistakes. I would do some things very differently. I was not a perfect parent, but I did allow him to grow up with responsibility for himself and accountability to God and others.

Adults are accountable to God for their moral actions and to the law of the land for their civil actions. They are mutually ACCOUNTABLE to anyone with whom they have made a legal contract – as in a marriage, getting a bank loan, financing a mortgage or a car. They are RESPONSIBLE for themselves, for their own personal care, for their basic needs of shelter, clothing, food, transportation, employment. They do for themselves whatever they CAN do for themselves. Adults are like that.

Children, on the other hand, begin their lives being completely dependent on others. They cry and sleep and poop and pee ... and eat if someone feeds them. Gradually they learn to take care of their own needs, to explore their little world, and to increasingly do things for themselves. Parents nurture, guide, teach, rescue, demonstrate, explain, warn, discipline, punish, scold, entertain, feed, dress, criticize, boss, and control. Healthy parents should do these things only WHEN needed and only as LONG as needed. Healthy parents let kids make more and more of their own choices and decisions and let them live with the consequences. Healthy parents set their children free, cutting the umbilical cord, sharply.

Parents often are the ones who decide when their child becomes a real adult. Sometimes a child will jump from the nest before the parent is ready to let them go. They usually survive the fall. Rarely does a parent push a child out before he is ready. However, he too usually survives.

The saddest case is when the child is clearly ready to be made accountable and responsible, become independent and self-sufficient, but the parent refuses to set him free, constantly pulling the child back to the nest. Depending on the child's temperament, he may rebel and move far away, or he may allow the parent to keep him dependent and needy, unable to be fully accountable and responsible for himself, only occasionally looking and acting like an adult. Both the parent and child are perplexed and unhappy about these unsuccessful circumstances.

This "grown-up child" cannot keep a job, stay in a satisfying relationship, or provide for his own needs consistently. He is miserable, and perhaps he looks for comfort in alcohol, drugs, excessive food, gambling, or shopping. The guilt-ridden and shameful parent tries repeatedly to fix the problem, to rescue their child from his woes. It only delays adulthood. It may be that the parent loves his child to death - literally!

Parents who continue "parenting" their children into adulthood also unwittingly demean them, belittle them, humiliate them, and degrade them by doing so. These parents hold the key to the freedom of true adulthood which these "children" crave, but the parents refuse to give it up.

"How?" you ask. "That is awful and absurd!"

Think about the adult child as just another "equal" adult, not related to you. One old AA friend of mine said, "Take the labels off your relatives and look at them objectively." Now imagine talking to a friend the way you talk to your adult child, alcoholic or not. All the criticism, managing, manipulating, controlling, advising, scolding ... Please! If you talked to ME that way, our friendship would be OVER!

Now think about how some spouses talk to their adult alcoholic spouses. Same song, second verse, same as the first ... only worse! God help us all to learn this lesson before we love our loved ones to death.

Surrender to Win

Give up the battle so you can win the war. That may not be in the War Games Handbook at West Point but it works in the battle against distorted, insane thinking. Surrendering pride, that false sense of control, is the first step in AA or Al-Anon: Step One – "ADMITTED we were POWERLESS over alcohol, and that our lives had become UNMANAGEABLE."

Admitting defeat, revealing our powerlessness, and confessing that we can't even manage our own lives is surrender. But the good news is it is surrender to a power greater, wiser, higher, and stronger than we can ever be. Even better news is that He has never been defeated nor will He ever be! I am glad to surrender to the undefeated Power who is always on my side!

Besides, I lived under the delusion that I could control the problem, perhaps that I had actually caused it to some degree, and that, given enough time, I could be the motivation, the inspiration for my loved ones to stop drinking.

I was even told before I married my alcoholic, "You will be so good for him!" No one offered me the possibility that he could be good for me! He wasn't then, but after all these years, I can see that I was perhaps good for him and he has also been good for me according to the truth of Romans 8:28. "All things work together for good for those who love the Lord and are called according to His purpose." He gave me a wonderful son, and therefore a beautiful daughter-in-law and two incredible grandchildren. God blessed me real good!

Then I went to Al-Anon and learned the "three C's."

I did not Cause it.

I cannot Control it.

I cannot Cure it.

Humbling as it was to hear those statements, my stubborn pride refused to surrender, to give up my efforts at controlling and curing it because I was driven by such guilt for the drinking in the first place. I had to surrender the guilt and the idea that I had caused the drinking. After all, I could still hear the lines "That woman's mouth could drive a good man to drink" or "If you had to live with what I do, you'd drink, too." Perhaps good joke lines, but not good thinking.

Humility is the essential element in our success.
I had to surrender the idea of being a god-like creature who could have such astounding effects on others – I did not cause the drinking. I had at times contributed to the chaos in our lives, but I did not cause him to drink. Drinking is what alcoholics are driven to do by some "demon" inside of them.

I tried with all my energy and effort to control it – and I tried to hide it from that awful group called "they." I lied for him, covered up the bruises he gave me, perpetuated the myth of a "wonderful marriage." It was hell on earth, and we both contributed to the hellishness of it.

I thought my love for him would cure it. After all, my mother gave my dad an ultimatum before they were married – STOP DRINKING! He did. I thought MY future husband's love for me was at least that great so he would respond as my dad had. Not so. He drank more. My dad was not an alcoholic. My husband was.

I did not cause it, I could not control it, and I could not cure it. Only God could "restore me/him/us to sanity." And He did, eventually, when my now ex-husband humbled himself and surrendered his will. Alcoholics have a tremendous ego. It is very hard to surrender, but they must.

NEWS FLASH: those who live with alcoholics have even bigger egos because we attempt to change THEM, control THEIR drinking, and even cure THEIR disease of alcoholism which only their Higher Power can do. WE can't even change ourselves without the help of God.

Give up. Surrender, and win!

Teachers, Preachers, Podiums and Pedestals

I was never a cheerleader, but I was in the Pep Club, the group that sat in the stands together at the high school games and cheered loudest. One of the cheers I remember best went something like "Bill, Bill, he's our man, if Bill can't do it, Tom can ..." and naming all the players, including the coaches, until it got to "Cats, Cats, they're our men, if Cats can't do it, nobody can!"

I guess you could say that was my lifelong cheer, but it was the names of my teachers and preachers I would include: "... if the teachers and preachers can't do it, nobody can!" Sad but true, I had a habit of putting these men I admired on pedestals. I didn't mean to; I didn't do it on purpose. I didn't know any better. I just admired them and expected them to be a better human being – who would not disappoint me.

What a joke! More of my insane, distorted thinking! Let's be accurate. They did not all disappoint me and fall from their lofty perches. Many of them were indeed high quality people who lived by high standards and principles. Some of them were exemplary in their conduct and in their treatment of others. Many of them were intelligent men who taught me well in public school, college, and church.

Why these three groups of men? They were dominant in my lifestyle. I spent most of my time either in school or church while drooling over "bad boys" in the parking lot! I did not become a fan of any sports figures, movie stars, or rock stars. Except for being totally wild about the Beatles for about a year in junior high, I just wasn't much of a fan club member. Preachers and teachers were real people; I knew the athletes, singers, and actors were playing a role. I thought these real preachers and real teachers were more worthy of my admiration and adoration. And those bad boys – well, according to the music of the 60's, they were just misunderstood and very sexy!

I also put men on pedestals who are not teachers or preachers by vocation, but who have taught me life skills – how to be a better human being. I have had informal mentors over the years who have shared their wisdom learned through many trials. Ironically most of them were alcoholics, and I can see that they have come through the fire; I am awed by their recovery. I need to remember they are not cured; they are still recovering, not perfected. I have been told that only 10% of alcoholics recover for life and stay sober. I need to remember as well that I too have a disconnect between what I know intellectually is right and best for me and what I actually do. This is not a moral failing as I was always told, but it is a gap that we can strive to bridge. It is simply human nature struggling against our God-given spiritual nature.

Loving my neighbor as myself means I give them the same slack and leeway I want from them. But first I do have to love myself! And that's where those bad boys came into the picture. I saw myself – my image of myself as a female – as undeserving of the men I idolized, but perhaps that bad boy saw the vulnerability in me and took advantage of it. We were two people who had such poor self-images that we thought we deserved only each other, I suppose. Now I know that I want to be in a relationship with a real man with whom I feel equal and who feels equal to me. We cannot fill in the gaps in our character by attaching to another person who, we believe, has the qualities we are missing. Only my relationship with Jesus completes me. We need to be two 100% people in a relationship, not a 75% plus a 50%! On the other hand, I do believe in synergy – the idea that 1+1 = 3; that two people in a relationship can somehow be better together than apart. But two broken people cannot fix each other!

So what's the harm in admiring or looking up to someone? No harm to them, of course. It doesn't hurt them a bit to fall off that ledge. It only hurts the one who climbed up there to put the idol in its place. The god is never harmed by either its worshippers' faithfulness or fickleness. A god is above all that. The worshippers suffer agonizing pain when their gods are found to be flawed. Such was my pain, repeatedly. I am apparently a very slow learner in many areas.

Why did I need such idols when I have faith in a true God? It's not as if I was searching FOR a god to believe in! I had one – Jesus Christ. I think perhaps I was like the little boy who awoke in the dark from a frightening nightmare, and cried out for his mother's comforting presence. Mom came to his room, turned on the lights, and began to encourage him to trust that God was always with him, even in the dark. His reply was, "Yes, I know that, but I needed someone with skin on."

That's me. I don't know about you, but I need someone with skin on. I need eyes to look into, a hand to hold, a hug, and a smile – someone to share a laugh over a cup of coffee, to share our feelings, fears, and joys. I have faith in God and I believe He is with me all the time, but I am pretty sure God answers my needs by sending a real person with skin on.

Maybe the important lessons here for me are to be that person with skin on for someone else, to accept everyone as equal to me, not better or worse, and to do my best every day to be a good example – not perfect, just a human being trying to do my best. That's all any of us can do.

One AA friend reminds me that "most people are doing about the best they can on any given day" when I am discouraged by my own inability to "work my program." I will do better tomorrow.

One friend, when asked which famous preacher/writer he admired most, replied wisely, "I hold no man in higher esteem than any other man." Only Jesus Christ, my Higher Power, deserves that honor, in my opinion.

TLC – Time, Love, Courage

I love the phrase "Tender Loving Care."

TLC is greatly lacking in some people's lives but not in mine. My dear mother is an expert on TLC. There is nothing more soothing and comforting than her gnarled, wrinkled 84-year-old hand on my hand to make the hurt diminish. My adult son is never too grown-up to turn down a gentle back rub from Grandma. When he was little, my son said to her, "Grandma, your food is so good you must have sugar in your hands." Everything she does is done lovingly, tenderly, with genuine care. I am so blessed to have a mother like her. But I need to learn to show myself some of that same TLC.

It takes tender loving care – or my version of TLC -- time, love and courage – to live a life of serenity in spite of the alcoholics in my life.

TIME – time never does the healing but it does require time for us to heal. We need time to get the principles, time to work the steps and time to let them work in us. It takes time attending several meetings before even one slogan may sink in. Nothing happens overnight. No "fast food" fixes here. Most people prefer to believe the myth that there is a quick way to recover from a hang-over, but the medical truth is that time is the most effective. We do all kinds of things, some bizarre, to heal ourselves of pain-causing ailments. Some of them work, but most don't. Time is the most important part of the treatment.

LOVE – be good to yourself. Be kind; don't beat yourself up if you recognize you still have a long way to go. We all have a long way to go – it's called a lifetime. Love yourself like a beloved friend because you are your own 24/7 best friend. Love your alcoholic, too. Try to find a way to see him or her with compassion, to understand his words and behavior as symptoms of an illness.

How compassionate would you be if your loved one had cancer? Cancer initially has few symptoms, little pain, no blood or other outside evidence. See alcoholism as a mental disease whose physical symptoms can be hidden; dry drunks never touch the stuff, but are still diseased. Their disease exhibits itself in other obsessions, addictions, extreme behaviors, and distorted thinking.

Alcoholism is a mental disorder before, during and after sobriety! Remembering that it cannot be cured might give you more compassion. And remember, a sober alcoholic is still sick in the head until the distorted thinking, which caused the drinking, has been transformed.

COURAGE – one of the things I pray for every day is courage, courage to change, to keep looking at my defects, to keep trusting God when I can't see the next step to take. It takes courage to be humble enough to admit you are powerless over alcohol and its effects on you. It takes courage to look honestly at a situation, courage to accept it as it is, and more courage to take the appropriate ACTION to change myself. It takes courage to live in the solution, not in the problem, as one AA friend repeatedly tells me. The most courageous thing I have ever done is to look in the mirror and be brutally honest, without rationalizing, excusing, glossing over, or lying -- to myself about myself!

What it takes to live a life of serenity is TLC ... the Tender Loving Care of Time, Love and Courage.

Toxic Religion – Even God Hates It!

I keep thinking about how Jesus treated two groups of people differently. With one group, He was patient, kind, non-judgmental without actually approving of what they did, and always lovingly encouraging them to "go and live right." Sinners caught in the act!

With the other group, He was highly critical, at times terse, unresponsive, and even called them names! He called them broods of vipers, hypocrites, whitewashed tombs full of decaying bodies – these were the religious leaders, the leaders of Jesus's own religion!

I thought Jesus was supposed to show no partiality, no favoritism? Apparently He favored sinners! He said he had not come to save the righteous but sinners. He said He had not come to condemn but to save. He said the angels rejoiced more over one rebel who was rescued than 99 who didn't need to be rescued. He said He died for us while we were all sinners, still refusing to believe in Him.

I think Jesus would love 12-step programs! I love Him because He first loved me.

In my opinion, one of the greatest sins of the organized church has been its self-righteous condemnation of broken hurting people. Jesus sought broken people. He was attracted to hurting people. His friendship with them changed them. Condemnation and criticism NEVER genuinely and permanently change people! Some churches of today too often bury their wounded. If you don't measure up to the standards WE IMPOSE on you, you are OUT! That's like going to a hospital, sick, bleeding, and dying, and being turned away because you are sick, bleeding and dying!

Let's define some things according to how I see them:

"Religion" is a human invention God wants no part of. Religion is ritual, rules, and self-righteousness. It has an agenda alien to God's purposes.

"Sin" is a term which refers to accountability or missing the mark of perfection. Biblically, we can do wrong or sin against three entities: sin can be a wrong against God himself, against other people, or against yourself. It is simply about accountability FOR a certain standard of behavior TO a person or entity. "Sin" can be determined by a set of three questions: Is this a loving action or attitude toward God? Is this a loving action or attitude toward myself? Is this a loving action or attitude toward my neighbor [humanity]? If the answer is negative, choose not to do it. Never, never, never ask another person, pastor, priest, deacon, nun, rabbi ... not even grandma ... if something is a sin! That's akin to honor among thieves!! (Think about it.)

"Prayer" and "meditation" are similar terms, related to each other. Basically prayer is what I call it when I talk to my Higher Power; meditation is what I call it when He talks to me. Prayer is my attempt to connect with God, not to use Him as a genie to get my way!

"Evangelism," in my opinion, means aggressively, overtly spreading or carrying a message to others. It may be a bad message or a good message, a righteous message or an evil message. The best "evangelism" is by example: shut up and walk the talk!

"Happiness" and "joy" are sometimes spoken of in church as having vastly different meanings, but I choose to think of them in similar ways. I heard a sermon recently that technically joy is the power to be permanently unaffected by external circumstances, while happiness is reliant on outside circumstances, subject to ups and downs. I disagree. In my search for serenity, I discovered that a) both are choices, and b) both can be permanently unaffected by external circumstances. I can choose joy and my definition of happiness for a lifetime, 24/7.

"Salvation" is the BIG word in some religions. It comes from the root word "save" meaning "rescue." Personally, I believe my higher power is God embodied in Jesus, He loves me unconditionally, I am accountable to Him for a set of principles He established for my benefit so that I would have a more satisfying life, and He has a plan for my life which is always in my best interest. He always wants to "rescue" or "save" me from my stubborn self-centered stupidity if only I would trust Him to do so. MY God is always good to me.

"Confession" means simply agreement – with God, with another human being, or with anyone to whom you are accountable - that their description of your behavior is correct. You say I lied – yep, I lied. You say it stinks – yep, it stinks. Confessing sin means agreement about the nature of the action. God knows it all anyways; you are not informing Him of anything.

"Repentance" means that, after I agree about the nature of my sin, I turn away from it; I reject it as unacceptable. Repentance does not require groveling. It means I reject those words or behavior and recognize it as detrimental to everyone. It does not mean I will never do it again; it does mean I do not WANT to do it again.

Are we our brother's keepers? I prefer that "I am my brother's BROTHER – his equal." Yes, we are supposed to care for one another. I believe we must help those less fortunate with whatever means we have available. Statistics from the book Radical tell me that anyone in this country who makes $10,000 a year is better off than 84% of the rest of the world. Anyone making $50,000 a year is better off than 99% of the rest of the world. Americans are RICH! If everyone who had more than enough of their basic needs would help those who have less than enough of their basic needs, poverty would not exist. But Jesus said, "The poor you will always have with you..." because, I believe, He knew the hearts of men were basically greedy and self-centered. No one who is hungry, naked, and afraid can listen to me spout off about "God." Even Jesus said so. I can at least help one person at a time.

Must we convert the entire world to our way of thinking? Jesus said to "go into the world," share the message, baptize those who accept it, and make disciples [teach them to apply The Way of Jesus Christ, not your way]. As the Al-Anon and AA twelfth step says, "having had a spiritual awakening, I will try to carry the message and to apply these principles to every area of my own life." Walk the walk first and THEN talk the talk. No one can truly change unless they are ready to change.

Can we change people by talk – by persuasive rhetoric? We are simply to carry the message of HOPE not fear! The only thing we need to do is to be a good example and to carry the message, and let God do His thing. Research about human motivation indicates that guilt and fear are the poorest motivators for lasting change. Jesus drew people to Himself by love, acceptance, and Truth, not manipulative rhetoric.

Can emotions and feelings be trusted? Do I need to explain this? Emotions can be generated by false sources including my imagination. I choose to base my belief system on Truth called the Bible which has stood the test of time, on the testimony of trillions, and most importantly, on the effectiveness of applying biblical principles to my own life. The Truth works.

The essence of error – the worst thing anyone can do for a loved one – is to rescue and protect our adult loved ones from the consequences of their own choices. Until I realize that MY behavior choices are harmful to ME, there is little chance I will change them no matter what you say or do. In fact, I often "cut off my nose to spite my face" in response to this manipulation and continued making harmful choices.

Sitting in church doesn't make you a Christian any more than standing in a garage makes you a car. Change happens when we APPLY the truths we learn on Sunday to our lives on Monday! Church attendance does not impress me ... or God.

Worship is the expression of an intimate LOVE relationship beyond explanation or description. Jesus said, "Love [worship] God with all your heart, soul, mind and strength." Daily, not 11-noon on Sundays!

Toxic religion is detrimental to being healthy spiritually, psychologically, mentally, emotionally, and sometimes physically, not encouraging a genuine relationship with God. There are good churches, but being in touch with your Higher Power, or God, is a deeply personal, private, intimate love relationship that no sermon, book, lecture, or set of rules can create.

It's the most exciting adventure you'll ever have.

Trust Funds – No Withdrawals Allowed

When I was in fifth grade, some of my trust issues began to take root. It was then that I learned the truth about The Big Lie known as Santa Claus. I was having doubts about Old Saint Nick so I wrote him a private and personal note on Christmas Eve, stuck it in the branches of the tree after everyone else went to bed, and waited till morning. I didn't care nearly as much about the gifts as I did about the truth; my love language at work. I had asked him, "If you are real, write back. If you don't write back, I will know you are not real." As luck would have it, my well-meaning mother saw the note as she and Dad played Santa that night. She wrote a brief reply, using her left hand to disguise her writing, and returned it to the envelope in the branches. I was ecstatic! Like a "miracle on whatever street," I rejoiced inside, "He's real, he's real, he's real!" Later that year however, an aunt unwittingly revealed the truth to me in a conversation with my grandma. I silently cried, "Is anything real?"

That same fifth grade year revealed my enormous gullibility. I was a smart kid, got good grades, always at the top of my class. I will never know why they did it, but I think now perhaps I have never quite forgiven them. My also-smart girlfriends began to talk to me about the "rocket pool" one girl's dad was building in their backyard. They said when it was completed I was invited to come over for a swim. I knew my mom would never allow me to go so, on the appointed day, I did as the girls had instructed, planning on sneaking there after school without permission. "Pack a swimsuit and come over after school," they said. I did pack the swimsuit, and I did take it to school. It was all a hoax they had cooked up, apparently at my expense. I was devastated when, after they discovered that I had indeed packed a swimsuit, they laughed and laughed telling me there wasn't really a "rocket pool." I felt really stupid. Inside I cried, "They aren't real, they aren't real, they aren't real."

A decade and a lifetime later when I suffered the consequences of my first husband's alcoholism, I cried, "His love isn't real, it isn't real, it isn't real." I thought I could love him enough and he in turn would love me enough not to drink any more. What I didn't understand back then was that there isn't enough love in my capacity to change an alcoholic's drinking.

And when, after trying to get past my second husband's abuse of my son, his lies and deceptions, and his serious mishandling of money, and love him anyways, he threatened to kill me, I cried, "No one is real, no one is real, no one is real." That hurt me more than all the first one's misdeeds.

Trust is a difficult subject for me. I am naïve, gullible, too trusting. I have been all my life. I don't yet know how not to be. I am working on it. I am easily taken in by habitual liars!

One friend suggested that I have never developed "filters" which would help me sort out Reality and Truth from "just a man's BS!" For example, a man may use an exit line such as "I'll call you some time," but not literally mean it. It's not really the truth, not really a lie, just an exit line. I understand that.

What I do not get is when a man says he loves me, does he really "love" me or is it just a manipulative line to try to get what he wants? My trust issues get all wound up in the filters and I don't know what to believe. How can a man say he loves me and then deliberately hurt me? And please don't start singing "we always hurt the one we love..." Quite the opposite – we do not hurt those we genuinely love!

When I was in fourth grade over Christmas break, I had to have my tonsils out. I was hospitalized for a week; I'm not sure why so long. There I met a kind nurse who signed my autograph book: "Love many, trust few, always paddle your own canoe." I don't know her name, but I wish she had explained that to me back then. At age ten, I just liked the rhyme of it. I get it now, of course, but it is a truthful principle that I would have done well to have applied to my own life.

"Love many" means accepting others as they are; they have no need to change to suit me. Love at its lowest level is simply good manners toward everyone; at its highest level it is worship reserved only for God. In between is the kind of love we have for those closest to us. That one special love reserved for that one special person may never find me because of my trust issues, however.

"Trust few" is more difficult. It means I let only a few of them into my heart and into my head. My boundaries dictate what the criteria are for allowing someone into my life, intimately. I love the saying "come live in my heart and pay no rent." That means you don't have to do anything special for me to love you, but that does not eliminate my boundaries.

"Always paddle your own canoe" is clearer: take care of yourself. Do not delegate responsibility for your own well-being to anyone else. That includes your own happiness. It is not even God's job to MAKE you happy; "happiness is an inside job." This has been a very difficult concept for me to learn. Oh, I know it intellectually, but putting it into practice has been hard. I want to be taken care of; I want someone else to make me happy. I get weary of those chores. It's hard work to be this happy!

I am so eager to trust people even when, over and over, I am hurt with the trusting. And I refuse to let myself believe anything but the best about them for the longest time. My loyalty – my sick martyrdom – is unceasingly strong. I hung in there with my last husband for thirty years hoping, praying, and trying to make things change. It didn't. I hung in there with my first husband surprisingly long in spite of everything. I guess I have a sign on my forehead that only "sick men" can see: "Treat me any way you want to and I will come back for more of the same."

"Love many, trust few, always paddle your own canoe." Then "row, row, row your boat, gently down the stream - merrily, merrily, merrily [because this thing called life] is but a dream ..."

Work hard taking care of your own business. Be gentle with yourself. Be happy on purpose. And remember life is only TODAY. The rest – what we call "LIFE" and perceive as longevity - is but a dream. We make it up before it happens, or we remember it the way we choose. Memory and imagination – a dream. Life – the perception of longevity – is but a dream. All we really have is TODAY. The past and the future are both only in our minds – our memories of the past and our imaginations of the future.

Life IS but a dream. Today is reality. Let it go, my friend ... This is the day the Lord has made – rejoice IN IT ... NOW. THIS ONE DAY – this is your life.

Row gently.

Used Doormat For Sale, Cheap!

Newspaper ad I would like to post:

"For sale, cheap, one DOORMAT with lifetime use; years of wear and tear left; good for wiping feet in all seasons; no longer needed here."

A counselor told a friend of mine, "If you don't want to be walked on, get up off the floor." Funny how ridiculously simple that is to say, and how difficult it has been for me to do. Oh, I can get up when I'm down there – with a little help from a strong arm – but what makes me slither off my chair right back into the floor? A few choice words, a look, a thought of possible rejection will start me sliding in the floor's direction.

Don't get me wrong; I'm a strong-willed woman. Strangers have walked up to me as I stood in a group assuming that I was the one in charge there. I can take charge; I can lead and bark directions. My son used to say – thank God it's past tense – that I was an expert at "quality control." I'm opinionated (thus these essays) and

I can hold my own in a debate. I taught every grade level in school at least short term over a thirty-year career and no student of any age or size ever got the better of me. I broke up fights between teenage boys who out-sized me by 100 pounds and 15 inches. I am fearless – with children of any size, with sweet old people, and with most women!

But let a man say those charming words, give me that look, while even hinting, on the other hand, that he might also reject me, and I am silly putty in his hands. I didn't say "easy" in that you-know-what-I-mean context, but ... snap, snap, snap ... and I'm in doormat mode. The relationship will be almost entirely on his terms. We will talk when HE calls me, when HE decides to answer my phone call; we will see each other when HE decides we will see each other. We will go where HE says we will go. It is as if I have no say in what should be an equal adult relationship. What am I thinking? I am stuck on stupid ... again!

My girlfriend, who doesn't know what being a doormat means unless SHE'S wiping HER tiny little feet on HIM, told me simply to get up off the floor! I think she said it in Pig Latin, because all I said was, "Huh? What?"

Getting up off the floor, not being a doormat, or not being treated like a child, is done by standing up on EQUAL terms with that other person. It is done when I kindly but confidently say, "No, thanks, but I don't really want to go there/do that/have that/watch that/eat that."

It is done when, hard as it is, I don't pick up the phone every time HIS number comes up when I am busy, tired, or sleepy; I let him leave a message and I may or may not call back later. I know that sounds like game-playing; it did to me, also. But I must send the message about my boundaries - regarding phone calls and every other interaction. If he calls after midnight several times and I answer each time, he believes, rightfully, that after midnight is an acceptable time to call – because I respond by picking up the phone. If I do not respond, he will stop calling at that time. Could I just as easily TELL him when not to call? Of course, but the message of actions is much clearer, and I am not locked into a rigid "verbal boundary" I may later wish to move.

I have learned, in MY experience, that we teach people how to treat us by what we accept from them. Sometimes I send the message by how I respond. If you try to start an argument or a debate, my response teaches you what words I will accept. For example, I hate ridicule, prejudice and bigotry. There have been times when I have stood up against it physically and verbally. Most of the time, shamefully, I did and said nothing to express that I found it unacceptable. I wish I could have simply said, "You may have whatever opinions you want to have, but I cannot continue having this conversation." And then walk away.

How do I demonstrate that principle now? I choose a proactive response – I do not REACT, I RESPOND with a slogan or a memorized reply such as "Well, that's your opinion." However, I cannot do it in a sarcastic, antagonizing manner. It must be said with dignity and with respect for the other person.

Sometimes the message is sent by the consequences you experience. If you hit me and I accept it, (meaning I do not tell anyone or call out for help or call 911 or file charges at the police station), then you have been given my implied permission to hit me again. Hitting back, withholding sex, burning the beans, scorching his shirt, or telling my family or friends is not a clear message. Hitting is considered assault, a crime according to the law of the land. My response needs to match the action. An illegal action needs a legal response!

Substitute any other action for "hit" and you have a plan for teaching people how to treat you. I am not suggesting for a minute that you must always invoke the law of the land, but I am firmly suggesting that SOME consequence, some change in the conditions for the relationship, some moved boundary line, which is a clear "deterrent" for that behavior, must result.

Otherwise, you will have lifetime experience as a highly used doormat. I know. That job should be at the top of my resume'.

Who in the World Are "THEY"?

They – the usually nameless, faceless group of people I worried about all the time. Sometimes They had faces and names. That's what really worried me. I knew Them, and They knew me. But They never really came up to me and said, "Hi. We're They." So I cannot be sure They were who I thought "They" were.

I am not sure where I got the idea that I needed to care about Their opinions. What exactly were They going to do to me? Was there a place to which They sent people for breaking the "Law of Not Living Up to Expectations"?

Remember the words in that song, "Oh I wonder, wonder who, my darling, who, who wrote the Book of Love"? Well, I wonder who wrote the Book of Expectations? In fact, I demand to know! Who ARE They?

Why didn't They show up when I did good things ... to congratulate me? How was I supposed to know when I didn't mess up if They never showed up to say "good job" or something?

Hhhhmmm .... It doesn't make sense. They seemed to know everything I did wrong or was even thinking about doing wrong, but I never saw Them face to face to hear Them tell me I had done wrong or not to do what I was planning to do that was wrong. They just said it was . . . wrong . . . at some time to someone.

And I never knew why it was wrong. I mean, I have read a lot of books, the Bible, the Constitution and the Bill of Rights, and I know a lot of rules, but I never knew how to find out what They were going to do next.

So to whom did They actually tell these things? Did They tell my parents? It must have been in letters or by phone. But then sometimes They must have visited our house because I was often warned against doing certain things because They might show up while I was doing that thing They would disapprove of.

Others have asked these questions, but never got the answers. I think perhaps we were afraid of the answers – it might have required some personal accountability for our actions; it was easier to pretend we really cared what "they" thought. It might also have been a device used for imposing our standards on others, forcing conformity to our own standards.

I am so glad my crowd of "they" has dwindled to a couple of people; I once went to Florida with the open-ended option of staying there. My consideration was primarily could and would my son afford to visit me there? My son and his family embraced it and immediately planned a vacation trip for Thanksgiving to be with me. Others whined and complained. I cannot control their reactions. "They" have all but disappeared from my life. And . . . I am the one who sent them away! Bon voyage!

Will Power or Higher Power?

I never have quite known which power setting to use. Which is best, D1 or D2, high gear or low gear? Which setting on the washing machine is really best? H-C, W-C, or W-W? To wait or work? To pray or take action?

My problem is that same old "black or white, right or wrong" mentality. My distorted thinking at work again, as if gray does not exist, the idea that something can be neither inherently right nor wrong. There are certainly some concrete absolutes in life, some things that are always right or always wrong, but fewer than I used to think. The Bible has many apparent contradictions in its stories. God's law says not to lie, yet Abraham lied. Do not kill, yet Moses killed. Do not commit adultery, yet David took another man's wife. We need to realize the Bible is a book of balance; it might really be mostly grey and much less black and white. Yes, there are some absolutes in life, but most issues are left open-ended so that the principles of the Bible are applicable to everyone across the centuries.

Here let me suggest an interesting book titled A Purple State of Mind which deals with balancing black and white, red and blue, conservative and liberal, Democrat and Republican, Protestant and Catholic.

The idea of either my will power at work OR my Higher Power at work is distorted thinking. The first three steps in Al-Anon are crucially important to this issue. First, we ADMITTED we were POWERLESS over alcohol [or whatever], and that our lives had become UNMANAGEABLE." Second, we "came to believe that GOD [a power greater than I] could restore us to sanity." Third, we "turned OUR WILL and our lives over to the care of this God as we understood Him." I can't, HE can, so I will let Him.

Some of us are fixers, enablers, nurturers, movers and shakers in this world. We want to control things, run stuff, and be god-like creatures in other people's lives. What a joke! We can't even fix up, move around, or shake down the mess in our own lives.

I used to have the reputation of being a leader. I approached my involvement in any group from the point of view that I am divinely appointed to "make it better" – it was my calling, my life's purpose. In all fairness, we should try to leave the planet in better shape and leave the people we encounter along life's journey a little better off for having known us.

However, whether they are better off or not is really none of my business. It will be their concern and not mine. I am not in control of their responses to my words or my actions. They are. I am only in control of my words and my actions. I can leave them better off by being a little bit of sunshine in their day, not by being a dark cloud hanging over them!

So when I came to Al-Anon I came with an attitude, in part, of how can I make this better, not just how can I get better. I am a believer in President Kennedy's mandate to ask not what my country can do for me but what can I do for my country. I wanted to live that out in every possible way. Never mind that some groups were doing just fine without me before I came. As the old song says, "I got along without ya before I met ya, gonna get along without ya now!" I was clearly not convinced!

This is part of my distorted thinking, my insanity. I wanted to fix things and fix people! It is both a blessing and a curse to be able to see potential in a person. I had a gift for seeing what a student could accomplish, not just what he was accomplishing now. Some kids were working up to their full potential; many were not. They were the ones I wanted to inspire! Inspire, yes – fix, not my business.

I approached my own recovery with a goal-oriented mindset. Twelve steps in twelve months – snap, snap – I'm recovered. Not possible! It is a process of progress that ONLY GOD can accomplish. My role is to cooperate. I cooperate with God by asking every morning to know what HIS will is for me today and by asking for the power to carry it out. At the end of the day I look back and say to God, "I believe that what happened today was Your will for my blessing or a lesson"; this enables me to accept it without beating myself up with guilt and shame and regret.

If I really think I COULD have done better, tomorrow I WILL do better because God will give me the power to do better. My AA friend says that most people are doing just about the best they can on any given day. When we know better, we can do better. I must be gentle with myself and with others.

Essentially, I trust God to do FOR me and IN me everything I cannot do AND to empower me to do what He WON'T do for me. Philippians 2:13 says that God gives us both the desire [the will] and the power [the ability] to do everything He wants us to do.

The book of James discusses the synergistic power of "faith and works." I learned this truth from the movie, "Facing the Giants," which perfectly illustrated: give your very best effort but trust God for the results. The two key principles to remember are that God does not accept mediocrity or laziness; and I neither feel guilty for a bad result nor prideful for a good result. If I have not given my best effort and the result is bad, I determine to do better next time. If I have given my best and the result is good, I feel satisfied. Even if I did my best and the outcome was not good, that is God's problem, not mine! This principle enabled me to go from being unable to sell water to a thirsty man in a desert to having a top sales record in a local business! All thanks to giving my best effort but leaving the results to God.

The answer to which power setting I will use from now on? I will use the G-O-D power setting because it works best.

Worry – Put it off till Tomorrow!

Worry is the one thing God would say, "Put it off till tomorrow." One of the best books ever written was <u>Gone with the Wind</u> by Margaret Mitchell. Such a wonderful study about the heart of a strong southern woman during the Civil War. She faced hardship that she was totally unprepared to face, and she survived. I loved her method for handling problems [not so much handling men ...]. Sometimes she just had no ready solution. "I'll worry about that tomorrow," she would often say.

I used to attend a large church in the Dallas area where the pastor taught us that he scheduled his worrying. He had a specific time period every day with a definite start time and a definite stop time for worrying about everything he wanted to worry about. What a wonderful idea! I know what I would have done, however. He was apparently highly disciplined and not an obsessive compulsive person. As for me, if worrying for one hour daily would help, I'd worry for two!

Seriously, the idea was not actually "to worry," but to address the issues and problems that are concerns in a direct, productive manner for a reasonable period of time. Address them; look for solutions. If no workable solution could be found, leave it there until the next day's "worry" time.

Learning to apply slogans like "one day at a time," "take life on life's terms," "how important is it," and "keep it simple" have all helped me not to worry. What does worry accomplish? The actions of worrying – hand-wringing, face-frowning, belly-aching – are useless activities. My energy and brain are better put to use by thinking about solutions.

In fact, I am better off saving myself from some of that thinking, too. That kind of thinking often got me into the worrying mode; I thought I had to figure out everything! I over-thought, over-analyzed, and over-processed everything. I thought I had to "figure it out," that is, find the reasons the problem existed first or the motives for someone's actions. I am not a detective! I am not a prosecutor! I do not need to know the why of everything that happens. I just need to face the reality of the problem, accept its reality, and decide two things: 1) Am I the one who must solve this? 2) And must I solve it today?" As one AA friend says, "Live in the solution, not in the problem."

I have basically learned to think, "What problem must I solve right now, right this minute?" Usually I had very few things that had to be solved today. I learned how to procrastinate! As Scarlett said, "I will think about that [all that other stuff which weighs me down] tomorrow." The Bible says, "Sufficient for today is today's trouble." Deal with today's trouble today. Yes, of course, we must plan some things, but most of our anxiety can be alleviated by a change of attitude and a bit of flexibility.

It was startling to me to read what Joyce Meyer said about worry in her new devotional: "When you worry, it says you think you can solve your own problems better than God can." I have never perceived worry as arrogance! Only God is a gentleman and never rudely takes over unless I invite Him. He urges us in scripture to "cast our cares upon Him because He cares for us." God desires to be depended upon. My prayer now is only, "God, your will be done today and please give me the power to carry it out." I will do my best, but the power and the outcome are completely up to God.

Ya Gotta Save Your Own Ass – It's Biblical!

[Perhaps that word is offensive to some; I apologize, but the message would be neutralized if said any other way. By the way, the word ass, meaning donkey, is found in the KJV Bible, where the law of the Old Testament gave rules for saving one's own ass if it fell into a ditch.]

An AA friend related this story to me. There was a rather strange old fella in an AA meeting in Houston, TX, whom everyone just called Big John. He was a large man, but more importantly, he was not very talkative. He was intimidating to some AA members, but my friend usually asked him how he was doing every week. Big John's reply was cryptic. He simply growled, "Ya gotta save your own ass." Period. He didn't offer more. My friend said this went on for a couple of years. The same answer to the same question week after week. It perplexed my friend until one day Big John died, not understood, no real friends, but sober.

Suddenly the truth of Big John's statement became clear to my friend. That statement embodies the essence of AA's mission. No one else is going to do the hard work of saving you from alcohol; you have to do whatever it takes yourself. Enabling, rescuing, blaming, whining, excusing, manipulating, lying – none of the litany of never-works methods would do it. Sobriety and serenity are up to you. Ya gotta save your own ass, indeed. After all, it's attached to your own backside!

Said another way, we all have to "walk that lonesome valley" as the words to one old song remind us. My dad used to sing that song, usually humming a few bars and softly singing those words. Six people were standing by his bed when he went through that valley, but he walked it alone. Yes, spiritually God was with him, but as much as we all loved Dad, no other person could experience death with him or for him. He had to walk it alone. As much as our family wanted to keep him with us, we knew we had to let him go. How could we have prevented his leaving? Foolish thinking. We had to "let him go"-- we had to accept the inevitability of his death for our own sakes.

That was the lonesome valley we each had to walk. At the time, I was loaded with an antidepressant, going through menopause, dealing with a business upheaval, accepting diabetes Type II, becoming a grandmother, and denying the facts of my ever-deteriorating marriage.

That was my lonesome valley and I was walking it alone. YES, GOD was ever-present.

But like the little boy scared in the night, I wanted someone with "skin on" to comfort me. My husband did not have the capacity to be what I needed. He was never there for me emotionally to talk it over, listen to my endless stories of growing up with my daddy, to do what I needed. I cried myself to sleep, waking up through the night, sobbing, as the reality of Dad's death hit my consciousness again and again. My husband slept soundly.

We each have our own lonesome valley to walk. We each have to "save our own asses" at some time. The families of alcoholics become just as "sick" as the alcoholic, sometimes sicker. Children of alcoholics struggle with the effects of their parents' drinking all their lives. Children of abusive parents often become abusers. Obese parents often raise obese children. Angry parents often produce angry children. Generations of impoverished parents seem to be stuck in a relief system which was intended to be temporary. We don't do it on purpose; we just don't know how to be different.

My lonesome valley may not look at all like yours. Criticism is rarely helpful. Advice that says "if I were you" is never helpful. You aren't me. I am me. I have a unique set of experiences, character traits, beliefs, and needs. The truth is "if you really were ME" you would do the same thing I am doing!

"Ya gotta save your own ass." Walk your own valley. "Get the beam out of your own eye so you can see clearly to help me get the splinter out of mine," to paraphrase what the Bible says.

The best thing you can do to help someone else who is in a similar situation is to be a good example and to share: share your own experience, share your own strength gained from it, and share your own hope that perhaps I might find similar help. Notice it does not say to tell me what to do! Remember beams and splinters.

You Can't Make Me!

One of my favorite stories is about a little boy whose mother was trying to get him to sit down on the front seat of the car. Now, mind you, this was at a time when no one used seatbelts, toddlers stood on the front seat, and kids slept in the back window. Don't be shocked; we all did it. The mother said, "Son, sit down." He refused. Again she implored him to sit down. Again he refused. Finally, she used the do-it-or-else voice and he complied, reluctantly. But as he plopped down, he looked up at her and said, "I may be sitting down on the outside, but I'm standing up on the inside." I love that kid; too often I WAS that kid!

You cannot really "make" me do anything without my permission. No one can, not even God! God especially is very respectful of the free will He put into me; if He would "make" me do anything, He would "make" me be perfectly obedient, righteous, sinless, in every way just like Him. Quite to the contrary, He allows circumstances, pain, bumps in the road, losses, lack, rejection, even sin to become my teacher. His lessons are surefire, time-tested, and perfect in accomplishing His will in my life ... IF I allow those lessons to do so. He will allow me to go my way, be prideful, stubborn, and unteachable, if that's what I want to do. God is much more respectful of my individuality and self-determination than people are!

We have it all wrong! We try to control people, try to MAKE them do things that we want them to do. Is it because we unconsciously have a desire to be "god-like"? But GOD is not like that at all! GOD is so accepting, lenient almost in one sense of the word, confident in His own power. He COULD make me do things, be what He wants me to be, but He does not. He is merciful, full of grace, unwilling for anyone to perish. God has been given a bad rap for sure. People are not at all good at imitating God.

When I was a little kid and I cried because I didn't get my way, my mother would say, "Dry up those tears or I'll give you something to cry about." That certainly motivated me temporarily to do what she said, but it was indeed temporary. Fear, threats, guilt, rejection, manipulation and deprivation are effective in "making" people do things. It is how a Jim Jones was able to inspire his followers in Guyana to kill their own children and then commit suicide. It was why thousands of Jews and others marched like sheep to the slaughter in Germany. The human mind can be manipulated; the human heart is vulnerable; the spirit is a void yearning to be filled.

I was a stubborn little girl, full of spit and vinegar at times, not just sugar and spice. Most of the time, however, my mother only had to speak to me authoritatively, and I obeyed. My dad spanked me only three times, all for mouthing off to my mother. He always said, "Girl, that mouth of yours is going to get you into trouble." He had had a terrible temper as a child and had been warned of something similar. My mother could get me to obey with guilt trips, threats, and fear. She was particularly good at using my desire for approval to manipulate me into obedience.

She told me basic truths from the Bible such as "God is watching you all the time everywhere you go. Mother may not see you, but He always sees." It was her intent, I hope, to comfort me; that principle is there for a positive reminder that He cares for us, but it was also used to get a desired behavior. I was afraid of my mother and, on another level, I was afraid of her God. You see, if she caught me doing something "bad," she punished me. It therefore stood to reason that God would punish me as well, perhaps more severely since He was "way up there with those big eyes." Her intention was simply to protect me from the consequences of potential disobedience – the evils of the neighborhood. The real outcome was not in her plan. Truth was the neighborhood did have its evils which parents are supposed to protect their little girls from, not some "mysterious all-seeing eye in the sky." Perhaps that's why He made parents?

To accept the idea that no one can make me do something without my permission empowers me, builds my confidence, and asserts my self-esteem. It is a fine line which parents of strong-willed children must walk to protect their little spirits while breaking the unhealthiness of an implacable will. More often well-meaning parents squelch in those children a spirit that should have been cultivated, nurtured, and freed.

I wanted to be a free spirit, but I was tethered to rigid rules. I am now finding my wings.

When I whine, my AA friend says, "You can whine if you want to, you can be depressed if you want to, you can be angry if you want to. But you can also CHOOSE to be content, to be happy, to accept life on life's terms."

No one can make me do anything!

I get to choose!